# From Why to Worship

Jonathan Lamb's royalties from the sale of this title will go towards the work of Langham Preaching, a ministry committed to encouraging a new generation of preachers and teachers around the world. For more information, see www.langhampartnership.org or write to the author at Langham Preaching, 16 Eden Drive, Oxford OX3 0AB, England.

# From Why to Worship

A journey through the prophecy of Habakkuk

Jonathan Lamb

LONDON ● COLORADO SPRINGS ● HYDERABAD

13  12  11  10  09  08  07    7  6  5  4  3  2  1

First published 2007 by Authentic Media
9 Holdom Avenue, Bletchley, Milton Keynes, Bucks, MK1 1QR, UK
1820 Jet Stream Drive, Colorado Springs, CO 80921, USA
OM Authentic Media, Medchal Road, Jeedimetla Village,
Secunderabad 500 055, A.P., India
www.authenticmedia.co.uk
Authentic Media is a division of IBS-STL UK, a company limited by
guarantee (registered charity no. 270162)

**British Library Cataloguing in Publication Data**

A catalogue record for this book is available from the
British Library

ISBN-13: 978-1-85078-747-1
ISBN-10: 1-85078-747-6

Cover Design by fourninezero design.
Print Management by Adare Carwin
Printed and bound in Great Britain by J.H. Haynes & Co., Sparkford

*Dedication*

To the families of Gary Cross, John Bell, Femi Adeleye, Haward Beckett, Dave Rousseau, Chris Anderson, Asafa M'kana, Ann Mitchell and Annette Pitchford, representatives of the Christian community in Zimbabwe who are demonstrating Habakkuk's resilient faith.

# Contents

The aim of this study guide                                              ix

Preface                                                                  xi

■ SECTION 1  WHY?                        Habakkuk 1:1-17        1

Chapter 1     Habakkuk's problem         Habakkuk 1:1-11        6

Chapter 2     Habakkuk's perplexity      Habakkuk 1:12-17      18

■ SECTION 2  WAIT!                       Habakkuk 2:1-5        29

Chapter 3     Careful listening          Habakkuk 2:1-3        33

Chapter 4     Patient waiting            Habakkuk 2:3-5        43

■ SECTION 3  WOE!                        Habakkuk 2:6-20       55

Chapter 5     The certainty of God's judgement   Habakkuk 2:6-20   59

Chapter 6     The certainty of God's rule        Habakkuk 2:14,20  75

■ SECTION 4  WATCH!                      Habakkuk 3:1-15       83

Chapter 7     Habakkuk's appeal          Habakkuk 3:1,2        88

Chapter 8     Habakkuk's vision          Habakkuk 3:3-15       96

■ SECTION 5  WORSHIP!                    Habakkuk 3:16-19     109

Chapter 9     Respect for the Lord       Habakkuk 3:16        113

Chapter 10    Rejoice in the Lord        Habakkuk 3:17-19     121

## THE AIM OF THIS STUDY GUIDE

In this study guide Jonathan Lamb unpacks the book of Habakkuk. Habakkuk is only three chapters long and so the study guide covers every major section of the prophecy, often spending time exploring a key verse or short phrase. It is important to try and capture the sweep of the whole book, since it represents something of a spiritual pilgrimage for Habakkuk – and perhaps for us too. So although we might be more familiar with certain sections, it is worth working through the book systematically because Habakkuk's strong declarations of faith and worship at the end of the book are all the more impressive once we have taken the journey with him.

The questions in each chapter help relate the principles explained in the commentary to our own lives and situations. You can use this guide either for your own devotional time with God or as a part of a group. Enjoy your study.

## USING THIS BOOK FOR PERSONAL STUDY

Begin by praying and reading through the passage and commentary a number of times before looking at the questions. You may find it helpful to note down your answers to the questions and any other thoughts you may have. Putting pen to paper will help you think through the issues and how they specifically apply to your own situation. It will also be encouraging to look back over all that God has been teaching you. Talk about what you're learning with a friend. Pray together that you'll be able to apply all these new lessons to your life.

## USING THIS BOOK IN A SMALL GROUP: FOR GROUP LEADERS

In preparation for the study, pray and read the passage of Scripture and commentary over a number of times. Use other resource material such as a Bible dictionary or atlas if it would be helpful. Before each session, think through what materials you need for the study – a flip chart, pens and paper, other Bible translations, worship tapes?

At the top of each chapter we have stated the aim – this is the heart of the passage and the truth you want your group to take away with them. With this in mind, decide which questions and activities you should spend most time on. Add questions that would be helpful to your group or particular church situation.

Before people come, encourage them to read the passage and commentary that you will be studying each week.

Make sure you leave time at the end of the study for people to 'Reflect and Respond' so they are able to apply what they are learning to their own situation.

# Preface

I am writing at the close of a year which has been widely regarded as one of the most turbulent in recent times. Whether it is the devastation of natural disasters, the fears of global climatic change, the never-ending violence of the Middle East and the Gulf, the threat from rogue states, the tragedy of Darfur, the underlying and universal fear of terrorism – each has contributed to a global mood of uncertainty and bewilderment. The Christian church has encountered additional pressures, with persecution impacting an estimated two hundred million evangelicals worldwide and with a range of challenges associated with religious pluralism and with moral and spiritual decline. Whether at the international or the personal level, all Christians at one time or another identify with Habakkuk's struggles.

These chapters were originally prepared as five Bible expositions given at the Keswick Convention in the English Lake District in the summer of 2004. The event was organised around the theme 'Out of Control?' and the short prophecy of Habakkuk seemed very appropriate, for it both articulates the questions which Christian believers ask and expresses the certainties which we must also embrace. Although the book of Habakkuk is well known for its memorable closing doxology ('Though the fig tree does not blossom . . . yet I will rejoice in the Lord'), we find no easy-believism or cheap Hallelujahs. Habakkuk had made a demanding journey from the bewildered questions and complaints of chapter 1 to offering the worship of a man who had discovered that, when everything is stripped away, God is enough.

I am grateful to Peter Maiden and the Keswick Council for their invitation to preach this series, which encouraged me to reflect on the foundations of faith in an uncertain world. It came at a time when, in our family life, we encountered a cluster of health challenges which, whilst provoking some of the opening questions which Habakkuk asked, also led us to a more settled faith in God's good purposes. I am specially thankful for the support of my wife Margaret and my three daughters, Catherine, Rebecca and Anna, who also made the journey through a demanding time in our lives. But we were also aware that our challenges were relatively insignificant when compared to the struggles encountered by so many of our fellow believers around the world. By way of example, I mention the country of Zimbabwe, which I have been privileged to visit in relation to the development of 'Keswick Zimbabwe' and the work of Langham Preaching. It is a country which seems to reflect some of the themes which Habakkuk is addressing: on the one hand, the steady deterioration of society (not least summarised in the closing verses of chapter 3 – 'the fields produce no food' . . .), yet on the other, the remarkable faith of the believing community, rising above the political, social and economic decline and holding fast to the Lord. It is to a group of families in Zimbabwe who supported the development of the small Keswick programme that I am pleased to dedicate this book.

The style and structure of much of the preached material is retained, but in re-working these chapters I have tried to ensure readability and also added suggestions for reflection and discussion which I hope will help the reader benefit from the same journey from *Why?* to *Worship*.

*Jonathan Lamb*
*Oxford*
*December 2006*

# Why?

## Habakkuk 1:1-17

# Why?

## INTRODUCTION TO SECTION 1

'At the start of the 21st century, humankind finds itself on a non-sustainable course – a course that, unless it is changed, could lead to grand-scale catastrophes.' James Martin opens his book on *The Meaning of the 21st Century*[1] with a sentiment which is becoming more and more familiar to us. Martin goes on to offer an optimistic blueprint for 'ensuring our future', but dark fears lurk in the hearts and minds of most of us. There is hardly a country around the world where this question is not surfacing: who is in control? What is happening to our world and where is it all heading?

Such questions tap into the mood of our culture. There is a frightening array of uncertainties. There is the sustained threat from rogue states: if there is military engagement in North Korea or Iran, then the ripple effects will be truly terrifying. There are questions about the clash of civilizations, the violence perpetrated by religious extremists and the moral confusion arising from liberal views of all kinds. Then there is the threat of global warming and, most obviously, the ever-present spectre of international terrorism: never mind the billions which people spend on defence and security systems, nothing can control this particular threat.

We sense that we have entered an era of bewildering uncertainty where no-one is in control. It is a fault-line in our world, a deep vulnerability that many people express. And it is not simply to do with global events. It is also reflected in a concern that their own personal world often seems out of control. I remember a conversation with a pastor of a London church who was honest enough to confess to this. He was seventy years old, fifty years a Christian, and had had a demanding pastoral responsibility in speaking to a young couple whose four-year-old daughter had died in tragic circumstances. It caused him to consider everything which he believed about suffering and the character of God. He was not bitter but he was deeply perplexed. He could not come to terms with how such a personal tragedy could sit alongside his understanding of God and his world. And many of us confess to the same experience. We realise that there are many things in this world which appear to contradict a bland confidence in God.

We are going to see from the story of Habakkuk that authentic biblical spirituality is not afraid to confront these hard realities. Habakkuk insists that this is God's world and that he is actively involved in it. All of us, sooner or later, confront a point of tension between what we believe about God's character and his purposes and what we observe in the real world around us. We frequently discover that our experience does not match our belief. Of course, we can live shallow Christian lives by keeping those two worlds apart. We can refuse to allow a two-way conversation between the difficult questions of our world and the certainties of our faith. We imagine that faith is best described by the schoolboy definition, 'Faith is believing in things you know ain't true.' What we believe and what goes on in the real world do not seem to match.

This point of tension is frequently presented to us in the Bible, whether in the wisdom literature, the Psalms or the prophets. And it is exactly the experience of Habakkuk. For like all true prophets, Habakkuk brings the word of God to the people. But what is especially interesting is that he also speaks *our* words to God. He confronts God with his confusion and, in so doing, he speaks for us. Is God really in control? As he looked at the bewildering circumstances in his world, how could Habakkuk be sure that this God was the God of the universe, the God who purports to be on the throne? As far as he was concerned, God had made so many promises to his people – that through them 'all the families of the earth would be blessed' – and yet they did not seem to be coming true. Habakkuk's name could mean 'to embrace', which is expressive of the way he took the pains and sorrows of his people to heart. It might also hint at his own wrestling with God as he struggled with perplexing questions of all kinds.

Yet Habakkuk is a book about God's purposes for his people and his world. In the course of three chapters we will see how God brings the prophet to understand that reality.

● *The mood of our age: can you think of issues which heighten the sense of uncertainty amongst those close to you, at work, church or home?*

● *The point of tension: do you agree that there is a point of tension between what we believe as Christians and what is happening in the world around us? Where do you feel this tension most acutely? Why do some Christians prefer to deny or ignore this tension?*

● *The nature of faith: we have suggested that often people imagine faith is a strangely irrational attitude – 'believing in things you know aren't true.' Discuss together some possible definitions of 'faith' that you could offer to a sceptical friend.*

Chapter 1 begins with a dialogue between Habakkuk and the Lord, dominated by the question 'Why?' The dialogue has three main sections, which we will examine in this and the next chapter.

# Habakkuk's problem

*Aim: to understand the struggles of a true believer.*

**FOCUS ON THE THEME**
If ever Christians are tempted to believe that genuine faith in God removes all doubts and questions, the book of Habakkuk opens with a dose of biblical realism. Here is a man of faith brave enough to confront God with his struggles.

*Read: Habakkuk 1:1-11*
*Key verses: Habakkuk 1:2-5*

**Outline**

*Habakkuk's problem:*
Carrying a burden
Calling for help

*God's purpose:*
God is at work
God is in control

## CARRYING A BURDEN (1:1)

A 'burden': that's the literal translation of the opening word of the prophecy, 'the oracle that Habakkuk, the prophet, received' (v1). It is 'the burden' he received. Here was a man with a heavy load on his heart and mind. Like all of the prophets, he received a word from the Lord which represented a challenging message for his times, a weighty prophetic word from a God of judgement. But the burden is also related to his burdened heart. It is very expressive of how he feels about what is happening in his own country, amongst his own people. It is there in the opening words (vs 3-4). 'Why . . . ?'

Habakkuk was overwhelmed by that question. He was living in Jerusalem, in the final days of the seventh century BC, after the reign of King Josiah. King Josiah was the great king who had introduced all kinds of reforms. He had had a conversion experience as a young man and he had discovered the law, pulled down the pagan altars and restored the Temple. There was a measure of prosperity and stability as God blessed the nation. But he was followed by King Jehoiakim, who quickly succeeded in reversing all of the good work which Josiah had achieved. Under his reign, the people ignored God's laws, yet still expected God to bless them: after all, they were God's own people. But gradually a terrible decline set in, a moral and spiritual deterioration which would have appalling consequences for the nation.

This was the context for Habakkuk's ministry. He was watching the steady drift away from God, the growing deterioration in the moral fabric of society. It is clear in the language of his cry in verses 3-4: 'Why do you make me look at injustice? Why do you tolerate wrong?'

'Destruction and violence are before me; there is strife and conflict abounds. Therefore the law is paralysed,and justice never prevails. The wicked hem in the righteous, so that justice is perverted.'

'Violence' was a word frequently on his lips. Habakkuk lived in a completely lawless society, shaped by the determination of people to forget what God had said and to live life on their own terms. They disobeyed his law, and prophets and priests alike were hopelessly compromised. As verse 4 expresses it, 'therefore the law is paralysed'. God's word was frozen out. Justice was replaced by anarchy. King Jehoiakim built his wonderful palaces, exploiting the people in the process, but he showed no repentance. And so the priests, politicians and civil servants took their cue from the king. They too became perpetrators of violence and injustice, adding to the moral confusion rather than resolving it. No wonder that Habakkuk declares, 'the wicked hem in the righteous' (v4). The few who did remain faithful to the word of the Lord were completely surrounded by ungodly behaviour which threatened to snuff out all signs of spiritual life.

Why was God allowing his people to act like this? Why was God making him witness it all (v3)? His was a burden of such disappointment and disillusionment that he was close to despair. Only God could help in this situation.

- *If you were to write a 'complaint' like Habakkuk, what would you say about your world?*
- *Are there times when your heart feels burdened by what is happening?*

## CALLING FOR HELP (1:2-4)

'How long O LORD, must I call for help but you do not listen? Or cry out to you, "Violence!" but you do not save?' (v2) This is the second feature of the opening verses. Habakkuk not only wrestles with the problem, he wrestles with God. There is an intensity in the way in which these words are written. They imply that he shouts, screams, roars: 'Help, Lord! Why is your law being trampled on? Why are you allowing people to drift away?' And it is important to see that the real crisis for Habakkuk was not simply the appalling deterioration he witnessed amongst God's people. The crisis was compounded by the fact that he cried again and again but it seemed that God was not listening (v2).

'How long?'
'Why?'

Those two questions are often on our lips. After you have been calling for a long time, it is hard to avoid the conclusion that God can't be interested. Why is justice flouted? Why is violence ignored? Why doesn't God intervene in judgement? In fact, we might go on. Why pray? Why have faith? We feel it as a terrible burden. As far as Habakkuk was concerned, everything seemed out of joint. It wasn't just the sinfulness of the people that was the problem – that was bad enough – but it was also the apparent delay in God's action. Indeed, it seemed somehow to be a blot on God's righteous character.

As we read the verses over and over, we begin to feel what Habakkuk felt. It was not an intellectual problem so much as a deeply-felt pain. And for sure, these questions aren't simply academic. As the novelist Peter de Vries put it, 'the question mark is turned like a fish hook in the human heart.' For many people, any explanation is better than silence, any reason is better than the confusion and uncertainty. At such times, it is very important to do what Habakkuk does: to admit our bewilderment. Contrary to what is sometimes supposed, Christians are allowed to do that. We often have great difficulty in living with such perplexing questions, since we feel we must have answers for a questioning world. We find it hard to live with mystery.

I wonder too if we have the same sense of burden as Habakkuk as we look at our own Christian community?

Or are we lulled into an easy-going acceptance of the status quo, a spiritual apathy which can so easily set in amongst God's people? I wonder if we have the same agony of spirit and honesty before God? It was Habakkuk's understanding of God that led him to shout out this complaint: 'If this is true about you, God, then why aren't you acting, why the delay?'

- *It is not easy to do this but can you describe to fellow Christians in your small group a time when you have experienced this kind of bewilderment? When God appears to delay in answering our prayers, how do we feel? And how do we cope?*
- *Would you agree that a sign of an indifferent Christian life is when we are not troubled by these questions?*


## GOD'S PURPOSE (1:5-11)

In the next section, God replies to Habakkuk. It begins with the word 'Look' (v5), which picks up Habakkuk's complaint in verse 3, 'Why do you make me look at injustice?' Now God encourages Habakkuk to take a wider look. 'Look at the nations and watch and be utterly amazed for I am going to do something in your days that you would not believe even if you were told' (v5). That is exactly what Habakkuk needed to do: to gain God's wider perspective. Notice two important features of God's reply to the questions that Habakkuk had posed.

### *God is at work (v5)*

First, God had heard Habakkuk's prayer. God was already at work. He was not standing by, indifferent to the concerns which Habakkuk was expressing. No, he says, *I am already at work if only you had eyes to see it*. The Lord was behind a series of devastating events that would change the course of history in Habakkuk's day. He had not abandoned his plans. Judah and all of the nations were still under God's watchful eye. He was providing a solution to the problem which so concerned Habakkuk.

> I am raising up the Babylonians . . . that ruthless and impetuous people, who sweep across the whole earth to seize dwelling places not their own. They are a feared and dreaded people; they are a law to themselves and promote their own honour. . . They deride kings and scoff at rulers. They laugh at all fortified cities . . . guilty people, whose own strength is their god' (vs 6,7,10,11).

It is a description of the devastation which the Babylonians were about to bring on God's own people. It wouldn't be out of place in our twenty-first century world. The Babylonians were guilty of international terrorism, ethnic cleansing and the exercise of ruthless power. This was 'a great military juggernaut' which crushed everything in its power.

Sometimes we have particular expectations of how God ought to work in our lives and our world. We think we know how our prayers should be answered. So it is important to note what God says: look carefully. Habakkuk *was* looking (v3) but now he needed a very different perspective. I once saw a cartoon of Charlie Brown, reading a book by holding it very close up to his eyes. Lucy asked him what he was doing. 'I'm reading between the lines' he replied. That's what we need to do. We must begin to see another story, to realise that beneath the surface stories of our lives or of our word, there is the reality of God at work.

Do you remember Paul's testimony in Philippians 1? He was confined in prison and, for an activist like Paul, this could have been frustrating in the extreme. But he wrote, 'I

want you to know, brothers and sisters, that what has
happened to me has really served to advance the gospel'
(Phil. 1:12). Paul was describing the way in which the front
line of the gospel was being moved forward. But how was
that possible? Prison was hardly the ideal evangelistic
platform. Paul's testimony highlights that, whilst he may
have been imprisoned, God was not frustrated. God was
at work. Paul was able to read between the lines; he saw
another story. For one thing, every day one of Caesar's
personal bodyguards was chained to him: four teams of
four soldiers – a captive audience. We know that quite early
on there were members of the Imperial household who
became Christians. The gospel was reaching social circles it
never would have reached had it not been for Paul's
witness, extending right up to Nero himself. Paul also
mentions that other Christians were encouraged to speak
the word of God more fearlessly (Phil. 1:14). So Paul had
eyes to see that, however unpromising the situation might
have looked, there was another story: God was at work.

Habakkuk had complained that the Lord was indifferent.
Now the Lord replies that he will show Habakkuk that he
is working in ways 'that you would not believe, even if you
were told' (v5). We often need a similar change of
perspective as we look at the circumstances around us.
Perhaps you belong to a very small church or are working
in a very demanding situation. Or maybe you live in a
country where the church is under enormous pressure, or
your personal or family situation exerts what seems like a
strongly restrictive influence over all you do. In all such
circumstances we should not lose sight of the true reality, as
God reminds us: 'I am at work.'

● *Can you think of other examples, either in the Bible or in*
  *contemporary life, where – despite appearances – God has*
  *been at work through unexpected circumstances?*

● *We have suggested that we need to learn to see 'another story', to 'read between the lines.' What are the ways in which we can cultivate this alternative way of looking at life?*

### God is in control (v6)

The second reality implicit in God's reply is that he is in control. 'I am raising up the Babylonians' (v6). God is not only at work, but he will act according to his own plans and purposes. Many years ago, Martyn Lloyd-Jones wrote an excellent small commentary on Habakkuk, in which he described God's decision to use the Babylonians in terms of God's 'unexpected providences and unusual instruments'.[2] That's certainly what Habakkuk must have thought. Raising up the Babylonians? In fact, this would be part of Habakkuk's perplexity, for God was implying that it was going to get a lot worse before it would get better.

What was so troubling for Habakkuk was that, although the Babylonians were in the driving seat of this great war machine, God was the Commander. Why was God doing this? First, because it was part of his discipline of his people. They had ignored his justice and so Babylonian justice would be what they would receive. If God's people were guilty of perpetuating violence and destruction, violence is what they would have, God replies.

The Babylonians were not just under God's sovereign authority, they were an instrument for God's purpose. These verses underline a very profound truth: God is the God of history. Hard as it might be to understand, God is even the God of such ruthless powers in our world. He is in control of the movements even of pagan nations. Calvin commented on these verses, 'It is not by their own instinct but by the hidden impulse of God . . . God can employ the vices of men in executing his judgements. The wicked are led here and there by the hidden power of God.' It might have seemed that it was the military prowess of the Babylonians which would eventually result in their success, but it was God who had raised them up to fulfil his purposes. God was in control.

It is vital that this truth settles in our heads and hearts. Exactly the same principle appears in the New Testament. The early Christians were bewildered at what had happened when Jesus was crucified. In their prayer meeting, they state that Herod, Pontius Pilate, the Gentiles and the people of Israel had conspired against Jesus. But then they add, ' they did what your power and will decided beforehand should happen' (Acts 4:28). The early Christians realised that the events in Jerusalem when Jesus was crucified were not completely out of control. There was another story. It was all to do with God's power, his will and decision.

The book of Job underlines exactly the same point. God granted permission to Satan to test Job, but God set the boundaries. As David Atkinson has pointed out, although there is evil in the story of Job, there is no dualism.[3] Some Christians appear to live their lives as if they were in a *Star Wars* adventure, surrounded by equal and opposite forces of good and evil. Neither good nor evil is quite strong enough and so this event must be due to God and that event must be due to the devil. It is almost as if there are two worlds of good and evil, with our lives swinging between the two. But that is not the picture that the Bible gives us. God is always in control, always ultimately Sovereign. Even Satan is under God's control, as the book of Job tells us. Habakkuk chapter 1 underlines that reality. God is saying, 'I am the one behind human history'. The Babylonians might think they are in control; the British, or the Americans or al-Qa'ida might think they are in control. But the rise and fall of nations and empires, of dictators and terrorists, is in God's hands.

We sometimes see this in specific global events, such as the Communist takeover of China in the 1950s. Thousands of missionaries were forced to leave but, in God's good purposes, the apparent tragedy of the missionary evacuation resulted directly in the extraordinary growth of the church, in a way that would never have been predicted.

It is also true in the midst of personal tragedy. Recently I was with an Indian friend who spoke about the growth of the Indian church over the past few years. There were various reasons for the growth, he said, but one woman ought to be mentioned: an Australian missionary called Gladys Staines. Mrs Staines was, until recently, serving the Lord in India. Her husband Graham was working amongst lepers and tribal peoples in Orissa in North India. In January 1999 he and his two sons were murdered when their vehicle was set on fire by a mob. His grieving widow, Gladys, told a newspaper reporter the following morning, 'I am deeply upset but I am not angry, for Jesus has taught us how to love our enemies.' Her words were carried in all of the Indian dailies, across the country and around the world. Hundreds of people asked the question 'Why are you Christians different?'

My friend Ivan charts the remarkable growth of the church, at least in part, to the brave witness arising from that tragedy. Asian apologist and teacher Vinoth Ramachandra has said this: 'I cannot help feeling that a middle-aged Australian widow has done more for the cause of the gospel in India than all of the slick evangelists on the 24-hour channel networks now beaming into that country.' There was no question at all that the family and the church were overwhelmed with the grief of that appalling tragedy. Many people would have thought long and hard about how God's purposes could possibly be fulfilled in such circumstances. Some of us may be walking along a similar path. Events occur which seem to make no sense, and we wonder how on earth can God be at work. How can we say he is in control? Yet that is what these biblical examples teach us – whether God's word to Habakkuk, the affirmation of the church in Acts 4, the moving prayer of Job or the brave testimony of committed disciples like Gladys Staines. God is at work and God is in control.

● *We referred to the way in which Christians sometimes imagine that life is a battle between good and evil, with some events influenced by God and others by Satan. In what way does verse 6 bring the true perspective of God's sovereignty – and why do we find this hard to believe?*

● *Some people refuse to accept the idea that God is in control. They look at terrible events and their consequences, and can only conclude that God has walked away from it all. How would you respond to this? What are the alternatives if God is not in control?*

---

### FOR FURTHER STUDY

The questions 'Why?' and 'How long?' are found frequently in the psalms of lament. Read them through, noting whether they receive an answer or not. What do these songs teach us about biblical spirituality?

| | |
|---|---|
| Why? | Psalm 10:1; Psalm 22:1; Psalm 43:2, Psalm 44:24 |
| How long? | Psalm 6:3; Psalm 74:10; Psalm 80:4; Psalm 90:13; Psalm 94:3 |
| When? | Psalm 101:2; Psalm 119:82,84 |

Acts 4:28 states the issue for the early Christians, as they looked at the events surrounding Christ's death. What are the key elements in this prayer (Acts 4:24-30) which guide us in those moments when circumstances make it hard to retain the conviction that God is in control?

Take a look at Job 1:6-12. How do these verses help us to understand the relationship between Satan's work and God's control? Job was not aware of the dialogue between God and Satan, so what impresses you about Job's response in Job 1:20-22?

## REFLECTION AND RESPONSE

• There might be examples from your life, or from fellow group members, which demonstrate something of the struggle Habakkuk experienced and which you are living through at the moment. Bring these questions and uncertainties honestly to the Lord.

• There might also be stories, as you look back, where you can see how God was at work in your life, your church, or even in national and international events. Spend a moment reflecting on God's mercy and thanking him for fulfilling his good purposes even in the most difficult situations.

# CHAPTER 2

# Habakkuk's perplexity

*Aim: to recognise how faith and doubt, certainty and perplexity, can co-exist in the true believer.*

**FOCUS ON THE THEME**
There are moments when, despite the assurances of fellow Christians, we find it hard to make sense of what is happening in our world. At such times we need to find our way back to the solid rock of God's promises, in which we first believed.

*Read: Habakkuk 1:12-17*
*Key verse: Habakkuk 1:12*

**Outline**

*Confidence*
God's commitment
God's eternity
God's purpose
*Contradiction*

Habakkuk could hardly believe his ears. And neither could the people in Jerusalem. One of the worst aspects of their treachery was that they had lulled themselves into a false sense of security. *We are God's people.* They couldn't believe that God would judge them through the Babylonians.

Paul quotes from Habakkuk during his evangelisic work in the synagogue at Pisidian Antioch, in modern-day

Turkey. It is recorded in Acts 13:41. He proclaimed that everyone who believes in Jesus Christ is set free from sin, but then he warns them not to dismiss his message. 'Take care', Paul urges them, 'that what the prophets have said does not happen to you.' And he quotes from Habakkuk 1:5: 'For I am going to do something in your days that you would never believe, even if you were told.' It is a clear warning: judgement came to them – don't imagine that judgement will not come upon you.

It's easy for religious people like us to become careless, even to mock the idea that God could judge us. Contemporary Christians may sometimes be in danger of that kind of flippancy. But Paul implies that one day God will judge all men and women. He is the Lord of history. That's why the gospel of God's grace in the Lord Jesus should never be ignored. In Habakkuk chapter 1, then, the message is clear: God is fulfilling his word. And that is the issue throughout the book of Habakkuk. If God promises blessings to those who obey, he will keep his word. If he promises judgement on those who reject him, that will happen too.

- *Would you agree that in our generation we are prone to carelessness and flippancy when it comes to the possibility of God's judgement?*
- *Where does the balance lie between a sober recognition of these realities and a joyful liberation that arises from knowing that in Christ 'there is now no condemnation'?*

Yet the promise of judgement still was not the solution to Habakkuk's perplexity. After all, as a prophet he understood that judgement was inevitable. He had another problem, a deep perplexity. Instead of God's purposes being advanced, they seemed to Habakkuk to be going in exactly the opposite direction. The 'cure was worse than the illness.' It was the point of tension to which we have already referred. You can see the apparent conflict expressed in verses 12 and13:'O LORD, are you not from everlasting? My God, my Holy One, we will not die . . . Your eyes are too pure to look on evil; you cannot tolerate wrong. Why then do you tolerate the treacherous? Why are you silent while the wicked swallow up those more righteous than themselves?'

Verse 12 is what he believes; verse 13 onwards is what he observes. We could refer to it as an expression of both confidence and contradiction.


## CONFIDENCE (1:12,13)

It is intriguing to see that many of the psalmists and prophets set their hard questions in the context of their certainties. That's very important for us too. We may have all kinds of questions but we must ask those questions in the context of the foundation truths of the Christian faith. In the midst of our perplexity we should affirm what we know to be true. 'Never doubt in the dark what God has told you in the light', says Warren Wiersbe.

- *Make a list of the rock solid certainties that you would want to hold on to in the midst of the darkness.*
- *What Bible verses would you bring to mind that encapsulate some of these certainties?*
- *Have you ever tried memorising Bible verses or passages? Choose one or two of the key verses the group has proposed and commit them to memory.*

We can summarise Habakkuk's confidence with three expressions:

## God's commitment

First, Habakkuk underlines the certainty of God's commitment to his people. He speaks to God in direct and personal terms. 'My God, my Holy One' (v12). He is implying: 'You are the faithful, covenant-keeping God, I belong to you'. Habakkuk affirms a fundamental certainty for which many people long: the security of belonging. 'We will not die', he continues. That's exactly our confidence too. God will not let go of us for, whatever happens, we belong to him. God is not going to give up on his people. The focus of this verse demonstrates that the issue rests not on our capacity to believe but on God's faithful commitment towards us.

## God's eternity

In the turbulent world in which Habakkuk lived, he was certain of another reality. God is eternal. 'O Lord, are you not from everlasting?' (v12). He is the God who is engaged in history but who is also above all of its turbulent ebb and flow. Whatever the fears and uncertainties of our lives, God is the Eternal, the Everlasting. He is the Rock (v12), the one stable element in an uncertain world. If things are shaking in our lives or in our world, we must hold onto God's changelessness.

## God's purpose

'O LORD, you have appointed them to execute judgement; O Rock, you have ordained them to punish' (v12). Habakkuk realises that the coming Babylonian invasion is something which God has ordained. Other prophets, like Ezekiel, Jeremiah and Isaiah, also realised that international events are not random. They are all part of God's sovereign purpose. These then are the three positive assertions which underline his confidence in God:

*God's commitment*: his faithful care for those who belong to him
*God's eternity*: his changelessness in a turbulent and uncertain world
*God's purpose*: his oversight and control of all the events of history

● *It is often suggested that we live in a generation that thinks great thoughts about humankind and small thoughts about God. How can we rectify that in our lives and in our church?*

Habakkuk's example in this one verse is enormously important in our own lives too. As we encounter the turbulence and uncertainty of our world, it would be easy to lose sight of the convictions which Habakkuk has expressed. I give one illustration, which for me is very descriptive of the Christian life. It comes from my experience of sailing in the Sound of Mull in Scotland. It was an incredible summer – until we arrived in Scotland. The winds rose to almost storm-force but the skipper was determined that we would make the journey. We soon learned how to 'beat against the wind'. This is a manoeuvre whereby you sail in one direction and then tack to travel in another direction, working a sustained zig-zag movement. You make very slow progress but the remarkable thing is this: you are using the winds which are against you to make that progress.

It strikes me that this is a realistic model of the Christian life. Sometimes we Christians think that we must always be riding high on some success-orientated spirituality. But Jesus never promised us that. He did promise that whatever winds and waves are thrown at us, we will still make progress to our destination. God uses even those opposing forces to help us move forward. We belong to the One who is the everlasting Lord, who is in control at the personal and even the international level.

● *We have suggested that the picture of sailing against the wind is a realistic model of Christian spirituality. Can you think of other everyday illustrations that capture a similar reality – of progress in difficulty or growth under pressure? Can you think of biblical illustrations or examples?*

Habakkuk provides three expressions of his confidence in God. But as we have seen, there is a point of tension. Alongside the confident certainties, Habakkuk also expresses his perplexity. He is bewildered by God's reply.

## CONTRADICTION (1:13b-17)

If his earlier complaint was that God is indifferent or inactive, then now his complaint is that God is inconsistent. The dilemma is expressed in verse 13. 'Your eyes are too pure to look upon evil; you cannot tolerate wrong. Why then do you tolerate the treacherous? Why are you silent while the wicked swallow up those more righteous than themselves?'

Look at the instrument that God has chosen. If God is meant to be the God of awesome purity, why does he allow the ruthless Babylonians to do their worst? The suspicion is that 'if he uses them, he must be like them.' The imagery of verses 14 to 17 underlines their ruthless behaviour. Like a fishermen with rod and net, the Babylonians sit beside the stream that God has generously stocked with human fish. 'He gathers them up in his dragnet; and so he rejoices and is glad' (v15). Historians tell us that the Babylonians placed hooks into the lower jaw of their captives to lead them along with chains. No wonder Habakkuk is appalled by the brutality.

Perhaps that is how it seems to us. We're perplexed at what is happening in our world. 'Violence' is a word which is just as appropriate as a description of our day. Apparently there are between twenty-five and thirty wars going on in our world at any one time. Or take another revealing measure: a child in the USA would already have seen eight thousand murders on television and a hundred thousand other acts of violence by the time they are eleven, not counting the number of enemies they have already 'killed' in various computer games.[4]

We must add that we are bewildered by personal tragedies in our lives, which seem to contradict our understanding of God's character. Habakkuk's perplexity is not that he thinks judgement is unnecessary; he knows that judgement must come. His concern is this: how can all of the violence and devastation possibly fulfil God's purposes of righteousness? How is God going to use this in order to fulfil his promises of blessing? Not only that, but how long is all of this going to last? 'Is he to keep on emptying his net, destroying nations without mercy?' (v17). Is God going to allow this to go on for ever? When will order finally be established?

● *What aspects of life lead you to share Habakkuk's sense of outrage and injustice? How easy do you find it to turn these things into prayer?*

## REVIEW OF SECTION 1

The demanding chapter we have looked at highlights three features of true spirituality and it would be good to reflect on these issues as we draw the section to a close.

## Confronting reality

I realise that the issues of this chapter aren't easy for us to confront. We can resolve the tension that we have described by dividing our life into distinct compartments, with our Christian life over here and the rest of the world over here. We allow no two-way conversation. We keep our faith carefully protected, well away from the troubling questions of our world.

But there is no need to protect Christian faith in this way. Facing up to the tension enables us to find solid rock underneath. Such realism is a feature of what Jim Packer calls 'adult godliness.' In his book *Knowing God*, Packer says, 'Unreality towards God is the wasting disease of much modern Christianity. We need God to make us realists both about ourselves and about God.'[5]

● *Would you agree that Christians are not always good at being realists – about themselves, their world or even God? If so, why do you think that is? How can we live with our feet on the ground and our hearts in heaven?*

## Praying honestly

Here is the second feature of biblical spirituality. Habakkuk chapter 1 shows us that we should be willing for an honest dialogue with God. I like the way John Goldingay expresses it as he writes about another troubled believer in the Old Testament. 'We need not attempt to bottle it up because God invites us to pour it out.'[6] Habakkuk has that kind of honesty. It is false spirituality to imagine that we must not ask these questions. If we try to exhibit a brave and cheerful face before other Christians or even before God, when inwardly we feel torn apart, it is almost certain to accentuate our distress. It is a mark of mature spirituality to confess these things to God.

'This is not merely an emotional catharsis', Goldingay says, 'like crying one's heart out in an empty room or losing one's temper and taking it out on the cushions. It is more adult to say what one feels to the person one regards as responsible.'[7] Habakkuk is not afraid to do that. He does not hesitate to be honest with God.

● *Children are often better at being honest than adults. What can we learn from their attitude?*

### Affirming certainty

'My God, my Holy One . . . (my) Rock' (v12). Habakkuk is doing just what the psalmist does in Psalm 42. He raises the same kinds of questions, set in the same context of certainty. 'I say to God my Rock, "Why have you forgotten me?"' (Ps. 42:9).

Martyn Lloyd-Jones wrote about the subject in his book *Spiritual Depression*. 'The essence of wisdom is to talk to yourself, not to listen to yourself.'[8] That is, we should repeat the certainties of God's word, the rock-solid affirmations of faith. This is the discipline that we need. Like Habakkuk, we must rehearse the great certainties of our faith, founded on all that Christ has done.

C.S. Lewis gave this advice to new Christians:

Supposing a man's reason decides that the weight of evidence is for it. I can tell that man what is going to happen to him in the next few weeks. There will come a moment when there is bad news, or he is in trouble, or is living among a lot of other people who do not believe it and all at once his emotions will rise up and carry out a sort of blitz on his beliefs. Now faith, in the sense in which I am using the word, is the art of holding on to things your reason has once accepted, in spite of our change of moods.[9]

- *Habakkuk expressed his confidence alongside his uncertainty. Why do you think the prophets and psalmists did this so often, and how can it help us in dark times?*
- *How can we help our families, or new Christians in our church, to be realistic about the challenges of being a Christian in this world, whilst at the same time strengthening their confidence in the rock-solid certainties of our faith?*

Here, then, are three practical encouragements that help us to live consistently in a broken world.

- Confronting reality
- Praying honestly
- Affirming certainty

When we are in such troubled situations, it is very easy for our questions and doubts to overwhelm us. We need to remind ourselves of the certainties of God's word and repeat to ourselves the confident realities that we have examined. Habakkuk was a man of honest faith. If we respond as he did, even in the blackest of moments, we will discover that God is our Refuge and Strength, that he is the everlasting Lord. As we turn to the next chapter we will discover exactly how Habakkuk did this, as he planted his feet on that Eternal Rock.

---

**FURTHER STUDY**

Habakkuk chapter 1 might not be studied too often by contemporary Christians, but the themes he addresses are not uncommon in Scripture. Take a look at some of the other writers who express their honest questions and discover God's care in the process. Even though the mood might be dark, look out for the way in which the writer also affirms his certainties. For example:

Jeremiah 20:7-18
Job chapter 1 to 3 and 38 to 42
Psalms 42 and 43

We have seen how Habakkuk learns that God is in control of the movements of leaders and nations. It is worth reading of other examples in Scripture to see how often God is at work in these unexpected ways, supervising events in order to bring about his purposes. For example:

Genesis 50:20; Isaiah 10:5ff; Isaiah 44:28 - 45:7; Acts 2:23; 3:17; 4:27; 13:27.

# Wait!

## Habakkuk 2:1-5

# Wait!

## INTRODUCTION

Some while ago, I spoke with a colleague of mine who said, 'The only thing holding me together is perpetual motion.' She meant that life had become so pressurised that if she were to stop, she would collapse. It is part of what is called 'modernity stress' – we are obliged to squeeze more and more into less and less time. The idea of 'waiting' these days is completely counter-cultural. We are addicted to speed; we demand the instant.

Thomas Friedman, the *New York Times* columnist, has written that the key to winning in business is to 'get wired or get killed, work 24 hours a day from everywhere or get left behind. You see executives walking around with so many beepers, phones and pagers clipped on to their belts that they look like telephone repair men.' He continues with the suggestions that we now live in an age of what a Microsoft researcher, Linda Stone, called 'continuous partial attention.' It means that while you are answering your email and talking to your child, your mobile rings and you have another conversation. 'You are now involved in a continuous flow of interactions in which you can only partially concentrate on each.' And Friedman points out the bad news: you're never 'out' any more. The assumption is that you're always in, always accessible.[10] Finding the opportunity to step aside from the distracted restlessness of our world or of our hearts is extremely difficult but it is absolutely essential for the life of faith.

On a recent visit to the city of Budapest, I was taken by a colleague to the old city, high above the river Danube.

There was a wonderful panorama across the city. The air was fresh and clean and the lights of the city spread out for miles. My friend said she came here every so often because 'it restores your sense of perspective.' It's very easy to be consumed with the day-to-day struggles or become swamped by the mass of details, for life to be bounded by the horizon of our own activities. But we need moments when we refresh our vision and gain a wider perspective, to see our lives in the context of a grander scheme, a bigger story. That's important in any form of Christian service, but it is specially important when we are confronting challenges to faith, such as those which Habakkuk faced.

From the human perspective, so much of what we do seems to be completely futile. When we compare our work as Christians to the scale of international turmoil, or to the opposition to the Christian faith which is raging in many parts of the world, or to the fragility of the Christian community – the whole thing looks so insignificant and irrelevant. This is where Habakkuk restores our perspective. From chapter 2:1, Habakkuk begins to gain a vision of God and his purposes in the world. We will look just at the first five verses of chapter 2 and we will notice three basic disciplines which Habakkuk learned, which will enable us to live lives of quiet trust in the middle of this frenetic and fractured world. If the summary word for section 1 was 'Why?', we now turn to the word 'Wait!'

# CHAPTER 3

# Careful listening

*Aim: to learn the disciplines that are required to truly hear God's word.*

**FOCUS ON THE THEME**
It is never easy for Christians under pressure to sustain the right perspective on their lives and their world and to nurture a 'Christian mind.' Hearing God's word is vital to shaping this perspective but how can we do this when we live in a world of distracted restlessness?

*Read: Habakkuk 2:1-3*
*Key verse: Habakkuk 2:1*

### Outline

An expectant faith
A submissive spirit
A responsive heart

After all of the turbulent questions and perplexed doubts of chapter 1, we begin with Habakkuk's determined resolve in the opening verse of chapter 2. 'I will stand at my watch and station myself at the ramparts; I will look to see what he will say to me, and what answer I am to give to this complaint.'

Like other prophets, Habakkuk uses the image of the watchman standing on the ramparts above the city of Jerusalem. He leaves the city behind, climbs the steps that flank the walls and longs for a renewed vision, a restored perspective. And there he waits. Many of us find that the challenges of our world can sometimes obliterate our view of God. In fact, it wasn't just a change of view that Habakkuk was after. He was desperate to hear God's word. He longed to know what was happening in his world. We have already seen that, as a man of faith, he believed in God's purposes and God's control, but he was living in between the time when the promises were made and the time when the promises would be fulfilled. Some preachers have used an appropriate image: he was in 'the waiting room.' That's exactly where we are too. God has made so many promises, but what will be the outcome? When will he act?

Before we comment on the specific features of *careful listening* that are clear from verse 1, perhaps you are thinking that this particular feature of Habakkuk's spiritual life seems incompatible with the mood of Habakkuk's praying that we observed in chapter 1. Here at the start of chapter 2 he is quietly, patiently, listening. It seems a million miles away from all of the turbulent questions in chapter 1. But in fact these two things belong together. On the one hand, he *pours out* his heart to God; and on the other, he *waits* on God. These are the two poles of prayer. We find them in Psalm 62, expressed in verse 5 'Find rest, O my soul, in God alone (or 'My soul waits in silence for God alone') and verse 8, 'Trust in him at all times, O people; pour out your heart to him.'

It is helpful to see that both aspects of prayer are expressed by the same man. Habakkuk, after honestly expressing his concerns and questions, turns away from every distraction and waits on God. It must have been enormously difficult for him to have done that. We should not forget what was happening in Jerusalem at the time, a situation which provoked the sustained refrain of 'violence' and 'injustice.' But it was vital that Habakkuk stepped away from the turbulence of the city and of his own heart and mind, and that he now heard God's still small voice.

A psalm that reflects the same pattern is Psalm 73, where the psalmist confronts God with similar questions and pours out his complaint. Why is it that the wicked always seem to succeed and the righteous suffer? Why, God, do you allow this to continue? But then in verses 16 and 17 we reach the turning point in the psalm: 'When I tried to understand all this, it was oppressive to me till I entered the sanctuary of God; then I understood their final destiny.'

Like Habakkuk, the psalmist took time to come into God's presence, and it was there that his perspective changed. To what extent is this a feature of our own lives? I wonder if you identify with some of the questions that we looked at in chapter 1, and what your response is to those challenges? Sometimes we live more by the maxim, 'Why pray, when you can worry?' Committing these perplexities to God is one of the most important disciplines in our lives.

- *What are the causes of our inability to 'stand at my watch', to climb above the world and learn to listen? Can you identify the typical distractions faced by those in your group and how they might be overcome?*
- *We have mentioned the two poles of prayer. Does one come more easily to you than the other? Why might that be?*

But what does careful listening really mean? There are three features in Habakkuk 2:1-2 that are worth noting.

## AN EXPECTANT FAITH (2:1)

This verse implies an active, earnest waiting for God's word. But it also implies a measure of perseverance. He is standing, waiting for that word. These are very important qualities in our spiritual lives, both in our reading of God's word and our praying. You might remember the sense of expectancy in Jerusalem some years later, when Ezra stood in the city centre and read from the book of the law. It is recorded in Nehemiah 8. God's people had returned from exile and had rebuilt the walls of the city. Now, as they prepared for their new life back home, they were desperate to hear and to obey the word of the Lord. Their eagerness and expectancy is expressed in the fact that 'all the people listened attentively', and in the way they stood up when the book was opened, and bowed down in worship as they came into God's presence. They were ready to hear and respond (Neh. 8:1-12).

There is very little to be gained from reading the Bible without that kind of expectancy. Jesus' own ministry was frustrated when there was no expectancy on the part of his hearers. He began to teach in the synagogue and he was met by cynicism and incredulity. Expectant faith is the soil in which God's word will bear fruit, and this is an element of our spiritual life which we need to nurture.

It is one of the lessons from Habakkuk chapter 1. Although he felt the weariness of it all (1:2), Habakkuk kept on praying with perseverance and with expectant faith, believing that God would finally speak his word. Don Carson offers some very useful advice: 'Pray until you pray . . . Christians should pray long enough and honestly enough at a single session to get past the feeling of formalism and unreality that attends a little praying. Many of us in our praying are like nasty little boys who ring the front door bells and run away before anyone answers.'[11]

Even if it might be through gritted teeth, we should 'pray until we pray.'

● *Discuss with the group whether your church is characterised by a sense of expectancy as you gather to hear God's word each Sunday? How can such expectancy be cultivated?*

● *What do you think it means in practice to follow Don Carson's advice to 'pray until you pray'? What might help you to do this?*

## A SUBMISSIVE SPIRIT (2:1)

A second feature of Habakkuk's listening is found at the end of verse 1. The NIV reads, 'I will look to see what he will say to me, and what answer I am to give to this complaint' (2:1). But there is an alternative reading which says, 'what to answer when I am rebuked.' Or it could also read, 'I will look to see what he will say to me and the correction that I am going to receive.' Habakkuk was aware of how bold he had been in God's presence in chapter 1. It is almost shocking to see the way in which he addressed God with his complaints and his anxious questions, and so now, as he stands on the city ramparts, he realises he must be prepared for the Lord's rebuke, 'the correction that I am going to receive.' He had presented all of the arguments, so now he is submissive enough to wait for the Lord's reproof and discipline.

David Prior rightly observes that 'God looks not just for honesty but he also looks for humility.'[12] Coming into God's presence with patient listening requires that we adopt the same stance. In all prayer we must be submissive as well as honest, ready for what God is going to say to us and open to any reproof or discipline that may be necessary. Maybe you have heard the story of an announcement that was made in a missionary magazine concerning the former General Director of a particular mission agency who was retiring, but was going to continue to serve the Lord 'in an advisory capacity'! We are not the ones with the answers when it comes to praying. We are not in control. Coming into God's presence, in the way in which Habakkuk did, requires that we are 'teachable as well as frank', as David Prior puts it. We are to be submissive as well as honest, open to listen to what the Lord has to say to us. He will change our lives if we come into his presence with this kind of patient listening. That was certainly the case for Habakkuk.

- *What are the characteristics of someone who is teachable? How are such qualities expressed when we come to God in prayer?*
- *Why is confession an important element of all prayer?*

## A RESPONSIVE HEART (2:2)

Here is the third feature of Habakkuk's careful listening. We read in verse 2, 'Then the LORD replied: "Write down the revelation".' The key word in this exchange is the word 'revelation.' This is the urgent issue. It is God's revealed word that Habakkuk receives, and which he is told to write down so that the herald may run with it. And verse 2 points back to the opening verse of the prophecy, which describes the oracle or burden which Habakkuk saw. It was this vision or revelation which God was calling him to record. The words of revelation from God are the vital turning point for Habakkuk, as they are for all of God's people who listen to his voice.

If we are perplexed about what is happening in the church, by the uncertainties of the world or the dilemmas in our own lives, then the starting point is to strengthen our confidence in God's revelation, his authoritative word to us in all of the Scriptures. Men and women of faith believe that God's word matters. That word is authoritative, dynamic and life-giving. As we come to the pages of Scripture, we look at that word 'to see what he will say to me' (2:1). Throughout its pages Scripture urges us to have responsive hearts.

What is your hearing like? I don't mean the state of your inner ear or your auditory nerve. What about your spiritual sensitivity, your ability to hear God's voice? God is a speaking God and a speaking God calls for a listening people. Throughout the Bible, hearing God's voice is a very urgent matter. There is a very insistent piece of writing in Hebrews chapter 3, where the writer quotes from Psalm 95 several times. 'So, as the Holy Spirit says: "Today if you hear his voice do not harden your hearts ..."' (Heb. 3:7-12).

Calvin's commentary on this section of Habakkuk provides us with a lovely illustration.

> As long as we judge according to our own perceptions, we walk on the earth and while we do so, many clouds arise and Satan scatters ashes in our eyes and wholly darkens our judgement and thus it happens that we lie down altogether confounded. It is hence wholly necessary that we should tread our reason underfoot and come nigh to God himself. Let the word of God become our ladder.[13]

It is a very beautiful expression and it expresses exactly what Habakkuk did – coming humbly to God to receive his word. This is our task as well: to let the word of God become the ladder into God's presence, lifting us above the turmoil of this world so that we listen to God's will and purpose in Scripture and are determined to obey.

- *What do you think the following expression means for Christians in the twenty-first century: 'Today, if you hear his voice, do not harden your hearts'? How does such hardening occur? And how can such hardening be resisted?*
- *Can you think of some examples of how, in your own experience, God's word has become a ladder into God's presence?*

Many of us find the disciplines of listening a real challenge. In line with the values of our culture, we prefer instant results instead of the sustained discipline of reading, understanding and applying the word of God. But if we are to find stability in this uncertain world, this is precisely what we must do. Our thinking needs to be transformed. If we are going to live by faith, we must have responsive hearts to his word.

Let me quote something with which I strongly identify. John White writes in one of his books:

> Bible study has torn apart my life and remade it. That is to say that God, through his word, has done so. In the darkest periods of my life, when everything seemed hopeless, I would struggle in the grey dawns of many faraway countries to grasp the basic truths of Scripture passages. I looked for no immediate answer to my problems. Only did I sense intuitively that I was drinking draughts from a fountain that gave life to my soul. Slowly as I grappled with the theological problems, a strength grew deep within me, foundations cemented themselves to an other-worldly rock, beyond the reach of time and space and I became strong and more alive. If I could write poetry about it I would. If I could sing through paper, I would flood your soul with the glorious melodies that express what I have found. I cannot exaggerate, for there are no expressions majestic enough to tell of the glory I have seen, or of the wonder of finding that I, a neurotic, unstable, middle-aged man, have my feet firmly planted in eternity and breathe the air of heaven. And all this has come to me through a careful study of Scripture.[14]

We should also note the instructions which the Lord gives to Habakkuk. 'Write down the revelation and make it plain on tablets so that a herald may run with it' (2:2). Writing on tablets is expressive of the seriousness of this word of revelation. This is the message that needs to be preserved;

it is of lasting importance. Some writers suggest that it may also have been necessary to record it on stone tablets because it would be some while before the revelation would ultimately be fulfilled. So write it down, Habakkuk is told; make sure it's safely recorded, for this is a serious message. Perhaps the recording on tablets also brought to mind the tablets of the ten commandments. This is the vital word from God. The phrases also emphasise urgency, as if the Lord were saying, Mark my words, Habakkuk, this word will come to pass. He has to make it plain, verse 2 says, so that everyone can understand the significance of God's revelation. It must be passed on to others, for this message is for all.

The verse is very clear, then. God's word matters. It must shape our hearts and minds according to God's perspective, determining the way we understand everything that is going on around us. Eugene Peterson, writing about the book of Jeremiah, says: 'If we forget that the newspapers are footnotes to Scripture and not the other way round, we will finally be afraid to get out of bed in the morning. The meaning of the world is most accurately given to us by God's Word.'[15]

---

**FURTHER STUDY**
We have referred to Hebrews 3, with its insistent demand that we 'hear his voice.' Read through the verses in which these exhortations occur (Heb. 3:7-4:13) and:

- identify the Old Testament examples the writer draws on, and think about why these are so powerful

- identify what the writer suggests are important ways to avoid the mistakes of those he cites from the Old Testament

- identify the qualities of God's word which the writer describes in Hebrews 4:12 and write a sentence about what each quality means.

**REFLECTION AND RESPONSE**

In this chapter we have identified three features of careful listening:

• An expectant faith
• A submissive spirit
• A responsive heart

Spend some time in prayer, seeking God's help to truly display these characteristics in your daily Christian walk.

CHAPTER 4

# Patient waiting

*Aim: to understand what it means to live by faith in God's word.*

**FOCUS ON THE THEME**
Habakkuk is going to introduce us to the two ways to live. They divide humankind sharply, for they are the only two options: faith or unbelief.

*Read: Habakkuk 2:1-5*
*Key verse: Habakkuk 2:3*

### Outline

*Patient waiting*
An appointed time
A reliable message
It will not delay

*Steadfast believing*
Unbelief
Faith

Waiting is not something we are particularly good at in our culture, is it? How are you when it comes to waiting at the Tesco's checkout? Or in a traffic jam or the dentist's surgery? Waiting is not at all easy. As we saw in chapter 1, as far as Habakkuk was concerned, waiting for God's actions was excruciatingly painful. That's why he was asking 'How long?' He longed for God's purposes to be fulfilled. When will God's promises finally be delivered? When will God's word be fulfilled? For many people, the pain of waiting is one of the most severe tests in their Christian discipleship, so it is worth noticing three things from the Lord's word in verse 3.

## AN APPOINTED TIME (2:3)

Habakkuk was tempted to ask if God was true to his promises, if God had forgotten his covenant people. In chapter 1 he is reminded that God was at work. Here in verse 3 the Lord repeats the message. There is 'an appointed time' when God's word will be fulfilled.

We should not imagine that this world is out of control. God's word and God's promise will be fulfilled: there is an appointed time. He is in control of the course of history. The appointed time referred to in verse 3 is actually a specific moment. It is the alarm bell ringing. The ESV says, 'It hastens to the end', a word which is also used of breathing. It's as if this word is panting, yearning for the end, gasping like a runner heading for the finishing line.

Habakkuk can be absolutely sure that what God now declares about the coming judgement of his people *will* take place. That's the first circle of application, the immediate context in which Habakkuk heard God's promise. And, sure enough, it happened. God's people were carried off into exile just as Jeremiah predicted. But then the word of judgement was also fulfilled in the Babylonians, who were the tool in God's hand to bring about that initial judgement. They too would be judged. God's word had an appointed time for them as well. And we can go out in further concentric circles to the ultimate end, when God will finally act in judgement. Habakkuk is looking outwards and forwards to what the Old Testament calls the Day of the Lord, to what the New Testament refers to as the Day of Christ. There is an 'appointed time'. God speaks and God acts, whether in Habakkuk's day, our day, or in that future day when everything will be put to rights through the coming of Christ.

If, like Habakkuk, we are tempted to think that God must have abandoned his people or given up on his promises, then we too must remember to wait patiently, because 'the revelation awaits an appointed time.' I realise that this is often rather cold comfort for people who are going through difficulties. It doesn't always help for heart-broken people to be told to hang on, with the assurance that it will get better eventually. But from a pastoral point of view, it is very important to try and retain the longer term perspective. There is an appointed time. God is not mocking us with his word of promise.

In his book *The Christian Mind* Harry Blamires writes, 'A prime mark of the Christian mind is that it cultivates the eternal perspective. It looks beyond this life to another one. It is supernaturally orientated and brings to bear upon earthly considerations the fact of heaven and the fact of hell.'[16]

A Christian mind, informed by God's word, sees things as they really are. Hebrews 11 reminds us that Moses had the true perspective. He was 'looking ahead to his reward' (v26). The verb that is used means to fix your eyes on something, like an artist intently gazing at the portrait he is painting. Faith that makes a difference is faith that fixes its eyes on the ultimate, not just the immediate. We must learn to take the long view, for God has today and tomorrow under his control.

● *As a group, list some of the things which are evidence that we live in an 'instant culture' and try to evaluate how these examples impact our expectation of how God should work.*

● *Can you fill out the suggestion that 'faith that makes a difference is faith that fixes its eyes on the ultimate, not just the immediate'? Why do we find this hard to accept? What kind of 'ultimate' things might help us regain our perspective?*

## A RELIABLE MESSAGE (2:3)

The second feature of the Lord's message is this: 'It . . . will not prove false' (2:3). This follows naturally from the fact that it is God who is speaking. God cannot lie and so neither does the revelation. There is an absolute certainty about that word. From where Habakkuk stood above Jerusalem on that day, appearances certainly seemed to contradict the message of God's ultimate control. The opposite seemed to be the case. And it was similar for Abraham, told by God that he would be the father of many nations – appearances seemed to argue for the exact opposite, since not even a single child seemed possible. So the message to Habakkuk comes with this assurance: God is not stringing you along. He doesn't lie. 'It . . . will not prove false.'

Peter was going to say exactly the same to the cynical people of his day. They doubted that the Lord would ever come back, that God would ever deliver on the promises that he made. And so Peter stresses that what God has said is absolutely reliable. When God spoke in creation it produced results; when God spoke in judgement in Noah's day, no-one could avoid the resulting flood; and by that same word he will judge in the future (2 Pet. 3:2-7). It is a reliable message. 'It . . . will not prove false.'

Isaiah uses the simple picture of the water cycle – the rain falls, achieves its purpose and then returns. Isaiah makes the connection: as in the natural world, so in the spiritual world. When God sends his word, it achieves its purpose. 'It . . . will accomplish what I desire and achieve the purpose for which I sent it' (Is. 55:11). Little by little, then, Habakkuk is learning that God is in control. It is a reliable message. 'It . . . will not prove false.'

● *If God's word is dependable in the ways we have suggested, why do we so often doubt it?*

● *Discuss together the ways in which you would present the case for the reliability of the Bible to a friend who is cynical or uncertain.*


## IT WILL NOT DELAY (2:3)

Thirdly, the Lord reinforces the certainty of the outcome by declaring, 'Though it linger, wait for it; it will certainly come and will not delay' (2:3). In the context of patient waiting, this speaks of another of our challenges. It is to do with our timescale compared to God's timescale. Do you remember how Peter expressed it to those who were asking 'Why isn't God acting'? He quotes from Psalm 90, 'With the Lord a day is like a thousand years and a thousand years are like a day' (2 Pet. 3:8). The delay in God's actions might seem long, but God sees time with a perspective that we lack. A long time for us isn't necessarily a long time for God.

In fact we have different ways of viewing time. A week on holiday definitely doesn't last as long as a week at work. Five minutes in the dentist's chair can seem a very long time indeed. And as we grow older, time seems to speed up as the years pass increasingly rapidly. The principle here in Habakkuk 2 is this: learn to see things from God's perspective. God's time is not our time. We think that if God is going to do something to relieve our suffering, he must do so immediately. We forget the great stories of Moses and his forty years in the wilderness, or the delay of twenty years before Joseph was vindicated. But as we walk with the Lord, we learn the lesson that looking back with a longer perspective helps us appreciate that God's time is best.

In his second letter to which we have referred, Peter is speaking of the ultimate perspective which will end with a new heaven and a new earth. The vantage point from the end radically affects our perspective on the present, transforming the way we live here and now. Of course, it is possible for Christians to subscribe to the doctrine of heaven but to live practically as though this world were all there is. We can live as though there is no tomorrow. But that is not the perspective of faith. John Stott has commented on Psalm 73, 'If the men and women of this world live in the cramped quarters of time, we Christians should learn to inhabit the wide open spaces of eternity.'

- *Can any member of the group identify experiences when they have been able to look back and see that God's hand has been at work in the situation after all?*

- *Why is Christian hope not simply about the future but about life now?*

## STEADFAST BELIEVING (2:4,5)

So far we have looked at the disciplines of careful listening and patient waiting. But there is a further significant theme in these verses which represents a profound turning point in Habakkuk's prophecy. The issue for Habakkuk and for all believers is this: how do we live in the meantime, in the waiting room? We now come to the key verse of the whole book. It is a verse which acts as the watershed in relation not just to the story here in Habakkuk, but in relation to the lives and destinies of all men and women. It provides us with the two alternatives: faith or unbelief: 'See, he is puffed up; his desires are not upright but the righteous will live by their faith' (2:4).

This pithy statement sets the context for the whole book. It marks the contrast between the faithful righteous who trust God and, on the other hand, the proud, bloodthirsty Babylonians. It speaks of the contrasted motives of true and false living, of the godly and the ungodly, the Christian perspective and the pagan perspective.

The reply that Habakkuk receives through his careful listening and patient waiting will prove to be the ultimate solution to all of the problems he has expressed. And it is this: the fate of the righteous and of the wicked may be slow in appearing, but the outcome is absolutely certain. Evil will be overthrown. God's enemies will be punished and God's purposes will be worked out in history. In the meantime, the righteous have to keep on trusting God. Let's look at the two possible attitudes which are placed before us.

## UNBELIEF (2:4,5)

Habakkuk's description of the ungodly is in verse 4. 'See, he is puffed up; his desires are not upright.' Such people are inflated with pride. They are completely self-reliant and that, of course, is why they are unable to find a righteousness outside of themselves. They live their lives in a completely self-contained way, imagining that they have need of nothing. It is quite the opposite of Jesus' opening beatitude: 'Blessed are those who know their need of God.'

The ungodly delude themselves in their proud independence; 'indeed, wine betrays him; he is arrogant and never at rest. Because he is as greedy as the grave and like death is never satisfied, he gathers to himself all the nations and takes captive all the peoples' (2:5). Proud and arrogant, they are never at rest – some translations say, 'he is never at home.' He is restless with his consuming ambition to get more. Nothing will satisfy him. Verse 5 explains that, like death itself, the ungodly person or nation just can't get enough. Here there is an echo of the description of the Babylonians in chapter 1, swallowing up nations to satisfy their greedy appetite (vs 15 to 17).

We are given a sketch in verses 4 and 5 of what we will see in the rest of chapter 2. It is a picture of the self-contained, self-obsessed person who shakes his little fist at God and says, I have no need of you. Such a person is living a lie.

- *Is self-sufficiency a characteristic only of the non-believer? And how about restlessness (v5)? Why are these attitudes incompatible with a life of faith?*
- *Why do you think Jesus opened his manifesto of the Kingdom of God with the simple beatitude, 'Blessed are those who know their need of God'? What does that attitude look like in real life?*


## FAITH (2:4)

'But the righteous will live by their faith' (v4). The righteous are those who lay aside their self-reliance and steadily look to God, completely committed to him. Their life is characterised by steady perseverance, trusting in God and his purposes. They live by faith, not by sight. Habakkuk's phrase is used in several New Testament passages to express the heart of the Christian gospel. In Romans 1 Paul describes how all have sinned and deserve God's judgement. Justification is based not on what we do but on what is done, for Jew and Gentile alike. 'For in the gospel a righteousness from God is revealed, a righteousness that is by faith from first to last, just as it is written: "The righteous will live by faith"' (Rom. 1:17).

Similarly, in Galatians 3 Paul asks how Abraham was made righteous. It was not through careful obedience to the law. No, a person is reckoned by God to be righteous on the basis of faith. We are justified freely by his grace. It is by faith in Christ's work on the cross that we are made right with God, and we can see how this attitude represents the exact opposite of the proud, self-sufficient unbeliever. We come to God aware that we have nothing to contribute. As Emil Brunner once said, 'All other religions but the gospel save us the ultimate humiliation of being stripped naked before God.'

Habakkuk came to see that the attitude of steadfast faith is the only way to live. It is to recognise that the whole of your life is in God's hands. The writer to the Hebrews also quotes from Habakkuk 2:4, demonstrating that such faith is a matter of perseverance, waiting for what God has promised (Heb. 10:35-39). 'He who is coming will come and will not delay' says the writer, changing Habakkuk 2:3 from 'it' to 'he' – '*He* who is coming . . . will not delay'! Faith is a matter of holding on to the Lord Jesus, trusting him day by day and looking for his return. The writer urges us to trust God that the Coming One will ultimately arrive. '"He who is coming will come and will not delay (quoting Hab. 2:3). But my righteous one will live by faith (quoting Hab. 2:4). And if he shrinks back, I will not be pleased with him." But we are not of those who shrink back and are destroyed but of those who believe and are saved.'

Christian believers are encouraged not to let go, for faith is a matter of perseverance. Hold on to the Lord Jesus, trust in him as you wait for the day of his return. Faith not only involves the initial act of believing when we receive the gospel of God's grace but it is also the steady perseverance of faithfulness. We depend entirely on him and we are to live day by day under the controlling principle that God is absolutely true to what he has said. The word of the Lord, to Habakkuk and to all believers, is that the only way to live is by wholehearted trust in the God who rules the entire universe.

- *Paul wrote that 'we live by faith, not sight.' What did he mean? (The context is 2 Corinthians 4:16-5:10)*
- *Why do you think this simple phrase 'the righteous will live by his faith' sums up the uniqueness of Christian belief?*

## REVIEW OF SECTION 2

We have seen from Habakkuk 2:1-5 that we need to climb above the distractions of our world and be ready to hear God's word. This will involve:

Careful listening
Patient waiting
Steadfast believing

Each of these three characteristics is counter-cultural: that is, in our world they do not come naturally to us. Yet they are essential for a proper understanding of what it means to live as God's people in a fractured world. It is vital that we recover the disciplines of hearing God's word, holding on to his promises and living with faithfulness.

As we do this, we discover that we can trust God with our lives, our families, our future and our world. This was the attitude expressed by William McConnell, deputy governor of the Maze prison in Northern Ireland. Shortly before he was assassinated, he said, 'I have committed my life, talents, work and action to Almighty God, in the sure and certain knowledge that, however slight my hold of him may have been, his promises are sure and his hold on me complete.'

---

## FURTHER STUDY

We have referred to the New Testament passages where Habakkuk's key phrase is quoted. Take a look at each passage in turn, highlighting how the author uses Habakkuk's theme to reinforce a vital aspect of Christian doctrine. The passages are:

Romans 1:14-17
Galatians 3:1-14
Hebrews 10:35–11:2

## REFLECTION AND RESPONSE

Can you think of biblical examples where people had to wait for God's promises to be fulfilled? What do you think are the benefits of learning to wait?

Do you know people who have a serenity about their lives? What is so attractive about this? Is it just personality, or is there a spiritual reason?

Is it possible to live with 'careful listening' and 'patient waiting' when, for example, you are running a lively home, have several small children and a busy professional and church life? How do you find the space for listening and waiting?

Regular reading and study of the Bible is apparently in decline in many countries. Why do you think this is and how can we develop this discipline in our personal lives, our families and our churches?

We have emphasised the importance of steadfast believing and wholehearted trust. Spend some time reflecting on how these qualities can be developed in your life.

# Woe!

## Habakkuk 2:6-20

# Woe!

## INTRODUCTION

There is an old Chinese proverb which says, 'To prophesy is extremely difficult especially with regard to the future.' But there is no shortage of people trying to do so. Some are surprisingly optimistic but the vast majority of people who attempt to predict the future line up with the remark made by Arthur C. Clarke, well known for the movie *2001: A Space Odyssey*. He wrote, 'No age has shown more interest in the future than ours; which is ironic, since it may not have one.'

Many people share his pessimism. There is now a deep-set uncertainty about what our future holds. We are no longer optimistic about the future of our planet, about international stability, about our own nation or even our own lives. Perhaps this issue is one of the most significant in relation to the question which Habakkuk explores – is our world out of control? How do we cope with the uncertainties and the pessimism which so easily eat away at our morale?

As we have seen, the issue at the heart of the book of Habakkuk is the purpose of God. Will God fulfil all of the promises he has made? The rest of the prophecy from chapter 2 onwards is an assertion that all of history is being directed by God himself in order to bring about his purposes.

In the last section we looked at the key verse of the prophecy: 'But the righteous will live by their faith' (2:4). We saw that this verse not only set out the two alternatives, the two ways to live your life, but it also implied two outcomes or destinies. The two alternatives are to live life on your own terms, to be the master of your own universe and to live in unbelief; or alternatively, to live a life of faith. We saw that the ungodly will never be at rest, they are never satisfied, whereas the righteous will live by their faith.

So where is our world heading? What is going to happen to those people who shake their fists at God and who prefer to run life on their own terms? The next section of Habakkuk demonstrates that the Lord God, the Alpha and the Omega, sees the end from the beginning. As we have seen in the revelation in the opening verses of chapter 2, his plans will come to pass. There will be no delay, for nothing will be able to stop the fulfilment of his purposes. It describes an appointed time (2:3). The runner is heading towards the finishing line.

The next section introduces us to an extraordinary vision, not just of the future of the Babylonians but also of our world. It not only speaks of the ultimate issues of destiny but in so doing it describes what has been referred to as 'the wheels of providence' in history. We will look at this section by examining two certainties which the prophecy outlines: the certainty of God's judgement and the certainty of God's rule. The first level of application in these verses relates to Judah in Habakkuk's day. God's own people they may have been, but they carried no diplomatic immunity. Judgement will come. Second, as we have stressed, the words of judgement are especially graphic in relation to the Babylonians. But we will also see how this ripples out beyond Judah, beyond the Babylonians, out ultimately to a judgement of all those who refuse to live by faith in the Sovereign Lord.

# CHAPTER 5

# The certainty of God's judgement

*Aim: to grasp God's evaluation of human unbelief and pride.*

**FOCUS ON THE THEME**
We enter a stage in Habakkuk's journey which was distinctly uncomfortable for him, in more ways than one. It might prove to be the same for us, because now we hear God's pronouncements of judgement. It isn't easy reading but as we uncover layer after layer of God's warnings, we will realise not only that this is an essential aspect of the Christian message but a vital theme that restores our sense of hope in a fallen world.

*Reading: Habakkuk 2:6-20*
*Key verse: Habakkuk 2:16*

*[Note: this chapter is longer because there is particular benefit in reading all five woes as one coherent message. You should feel free to take a break after the third woe if there is too much material here for one study – or if it is too demanding to absorb its impact in one sitting.]*

### Outline

*The certainty of God's judgement*
Woe against selfish ambition
Woe against false security
Woe against ruthless power
Woe against shameless exploitation
Woe against foolish idolatry

The key word in the first section of studies from chapter 1 was 'Why?' In section two (2:1-5) the summary word was 'Wait.' Now, in the rest of chapter 2 the key word is unmistakably hammered home in the remarkable vision which Habakkuk records. Five times the word 'Woe' announces a further stage of judgement. It is probably a multi-layered expression, including the idea of derision and containing echoes of mocking laughter. Some think the word woe also includes a sense of mourning, as in a funeral chant, whilst others suggest it implies the anger of a curse, as in Isaiah's phrase, 'Shame on you.'

This particular section is referred to as a taunt song. In a very helpful sermon on the passage, David Jackman suggests that in our culture we are familiar with the idea: on a Saturday afternoon you can hear the 'taunt songs' on the football terraces, as the supporters of one side jeer at the opposition. The focus of the song in Habakkuk 2 is the Babylonians, but we should hold in our minds the key verse in Habakkuk 2:4. If this verse sets out the two alternatives of faith and unbelief, it also hints at the two outcomes or destinies. The taunt song has something to say not just to the Babylonians but to all those who take their stand against God.

The 'woes of judgement' are not a particularly common theme in evangelical preaching today and, as we turn to this chapter, it is worth reflecting on our own reaction to the idea of judgement. Jim Packer provokes us in his book *Knowing God*

Do you believe in divine judgement? By which I mean, do you believe in a God who acts as our Judge? Many, it seems, do not. Speak to them of God as a Father, a friend, a helper, one who loves us despite all our weakness and folly and sin and their faces light up; you are on their wavelength at once. But speak to them of God as Judge and they frown and shake their heads. Their minds recoil from such an idea.

They find it repellent and unworthy. But there are few
things stressed more strongly in the Bible than the reality of
God's work as Judge.[17]

Habakkuk didn't have that problem. Indeed, that was part
of the perplexity that we saw in chapter 1, for Habakkuk
wanted to see justice prevail, he longed for judgement to
be carried out. But he feared that God's justice was
somehow unreliable, that violence would prevail.

It is worth taking a moment to reflect on the fact that
appeals for judgement are frequently heard in our own
world. Most people, Christian and non-Christian, are
looking for justice. It is a common refrain reported in the
media: 'Why do they get away with it?' 'Why let people off
the hook?' There is an appeal for justice. The people of Iraq
wanted justice to be seen to be done when Saddam Hussein
was tried in the Iraqi courts. Those who suffered under
Slobodan Milosevic in former Yugoslavia were appalled at
the prospect of Milosevic escaping justice, despite years in
the courts in The Hague. We want to see evil judged. We
want to see justice restored. We want to see order in our
society.

Perhaps that is why, in Psalm 96, the thought of the Lord
coming in judgement and final restoration is greeted with
such joy – 'let the fields be jubilant and everything in them.
Then all the trees of the forest will sing for joy; they will
sing before the Lord, for he comes, he comes to judge the
earth' (Ps. 96:12,13). The exuberance of God's people, and
even of the created world, arises from the fact that God is
coming to establish everything as it should be. Maybe that
is the perspective with which we should view the call for
God's righteous judgement. Nevertheless, judgement is not
a subject we consider without other emotions too. We
shouldn't read the passage ahead of us in Habakkuk 2
without tears in our eyes.

David Prior tells the story of D.L. Moody, the American evangelist, who was in Chicago holding a series of evenings presenting the truth of the gospel. On the first evening he spoke about the reality of hell and judgement, and told them to return the following night to hear about 'God's blockade on the path to hell', the good news of the gospel. That very night there was an enormous fire in Chicago and thousands of citizens lost their lives, including people who had been at the meeting. D.L . Moody vowed never again to preach about hell or judgement without mentioning the cross and the broken heart of God which took Jesus to Calvary.[18] It is from this perspective that we now turn to look at the certainty of God's judgement.

- *As we embark on the five woes, look again at Jim Packer's assessment of how people respond to the idea of God as Judge. Is this an accurate description of typical Christian thinking and, if so, why do you think this has happened?*

- *Why do you think that, for Christian and non-Christian alike, there are so many voices in our world which appeal for justice?*

- *Why do you think that we rarely read chapters like Habakkuk 2 and, when we do, our eyes are not wet with tears?*

## THE FIRST WOE: SELFISH AMBITION

### Habakkuk 2:6-8

'Woe to him who piles up stolen goods and makes himself wealthy by extortion!' (vs 6,7). The Babylonians were well known for greed and injustice. They robbed other nations and accumulated more and more by trampling on others.

They feathered their own nests at the expense of everybody else. It's a good example of what Habakkuk said in chapter 2 verse 5, where he described the ungodly as constantly wanting more. Most of us are familiar with that, for it is really the creed of our own day – grab all you can, look after number one. We are driven to want more and more, without regard for those we might injure in the process.

The outcome is described in verse 7. The proud Babylonians might think they are invincible; they might seem triumphant as they mock God, but will they get away with it? Is it all out of control? The answer is clear from verse 7. 'Will not your debtors suddenly arise? Will they not wake up and make you tremble? Then you will become their victim.' This is the device that we will see used throughout the taunt song: the Lord will turn the tables. The plunderer will be plundered (v8). A time will come when Babylon will be judged, just as the Lord predicted. It is recorded in Daniel chapter 5. Belshazzar, king of Babylon, was feasting, enjoying the fruit of all his ill-gotten gains, when the finger of God began writing on the wall. 'That very night Belshazzar, king of the Babylonians, was slain and Darius the Mede took over the kingdom' (Dan. 5:30). It is an important reminder for all who wonder about the apparent success of evil in our world, who might be tempted to imagine that the fat cats really will succeed. One day, God says, the plunderer will be plundered, the victor will become the victim.

● *In what ways might we be tempted to get caught up with selfish ambition, unjust gain or greed? How can we protect our personal life, family life and church life from these follies and from their consequence?*

# THE SECOND WOE: FALSE SECURITY

*Habakkuk 2:9-11*

'Woe to him who builds his realm by unjust gain to set his nest on high, to escape the clutches of ruin!' (v9) Here is another graphic description of the person or the nation who thinks they are in control. In reality it is a picture of false security. We know that one military manoeuvre employed by the Babylonians was to capture nations around them and thereby to create buffer zones to provide a measure of security. Though the tactics are different, the attitude is common enough today. People do everything they can to protect themselves against disaster. Using whatever means are at their disposal and with scant regard for the needs of others – not least the poor and defenceless – they build their imagined security with wealth. They think they've made it, they've got away with it . . .

Or have they? In verse 11 the Lord again pronounces the outcome: the stones of their buildings will give testimony against them. Those who have built their fortresses on the basis of ill-gotten gain will discover that those very things return to haunt them. Their schemes will back-fire, their great edifices will cry out for vengeance.

Nebuchadnezzar was enormously proud of his palace complex. In the outer courts the wall was some 136 feet thick, with each brick enscribed with the name 'Nebuchadnezzar'. And there is considerable irony in verse 10, 'You have forfeited your life.' Nebuchadnezzar of Babylon thought he had the whole world. But 'what good is it for you to gain the whole world yet forfeit your soul?' (Mk. 8:36). It is a terrible thing to get to the end of your life and discover you have completely missed the point.

Maybe the graphic image of the stones of the wall crying out is a hint of what would happen when God's finger wrote the damning message on the walls of the king's palace. Once again the message in Habakkuk's day and ours is plain. Judgement will come. The writing is on the wall. It is an inescapable certainty.

Think again of those two alternatives that we looked at in verse 4. Our calling as the righteous is to live by faith. So where does our security lie as God's people? My wife and I recently enjoyed going to a friend's birthday party, but the conversations there surprised both of us. For Christian and non-Christian alike, the subject of security dominated the conversation. I suppose it was because most of us were fifty-somethings confronting our mid-life crises and wondering about the future. But what kind of security? It was second homes, careful investments, early retirement, pension provision.

It's very easy for us to be sucked into the same way of thinking as the world around us. We may not be guilty of the excesses of Babylon or the evils of corporate executives who make big bucks through their shady deals. But we can get dangerously close to the false security of trusting the things of this world, instead of trusting the Lord.

I have a friend who works in Sierra Leone. He lived through the war in his country and witnessed a great deal of suffering. This is what he wrote, 'The only security we have is God and the only assurance we have, that which no man can take away from us, is our salvation. I am learning to look at what matters in life, not to waste time on things that do not have eternal value.'

● *It is easy for us to imagine that material goods, insurances and pension schemes are the real security for our lives. How can we live with a true dependence on the security of Christ and his word, when we have so many material things which support us?*

● *Do these verses have anything to say to big businesses and profitable companies which apparently make their money through the exploitation of the weak? What other examples of 'unjust gain' can you think of, which might also come under God's judgement?*

## THE THIRD WOE: RUTHLESS POWER

*Habakkuk 2:12,13,17*

'Woe to him who builds a city with bloodshed and establishes a town by crime!' (v12).

Nebuchadnezzar's palace would undoubtedly have impressed the tourists. The grand scale and lavish opulence certainly drew the crowds, but it did not impress God. He saw something else. One writer describes it in these terms

> Babylon's magnificent palaces, its costly temples, its grand processional street, aroused the awe and wonder of all visitors and its mountain-high walls forced upon them the impossibility of conquering this city. Yet the Lord Jehovah was unimpressed by Babylon's strength and grandeur. He saw only the blood of untold numbers of people who were slaughtered in ruthless warfare in order to obtain the means which made these buildings possible. He saw only the iniquity, the perversity, the crookedness of the builders.[19]

We should notice the chilling outcome which is declared in these verses, an echo of what Jeremiah prophesied about Babylon in Jeremiah 51:58, 'This is what the LORD Almighty says; "Babylon's thick wall will be levelled and her high gates set on fire; the peoples exhaust themselves for nothing, the nations' labour is only fuel for the flames."'

All of that effort in self-aggrandisement on the part of Nebuchadnezzar and his successors, the selfish ambition, false security and ruthless power: it all goes up in smoke. The psalmist was absolutely right: 'Unless the LORD builds the house, its builders labour in vain' (Ps.127:1). The word the psalmist uses for 'vain' is exactly the same word used in verse 13: they are working for 'nothing.' It is the same message that was recorded by the Teacher in Ecclesiastes. Vanity! Futility! They are working for nothing more substantial than a puff of smoke.

The chapter makes it clear that everything the Babylonians have done will be fuel for the fire of God's judgement. And so it will be for all those who choose not the way of faith but the way of the proud. We are back to the two ways – and the two outcomes. For the wicked, their world will be reduced to ashes; it will disappear in a cloud of smoke.

How can we be certain? 'Has not the LORD Almighty determined' it? (v13). If he is the Lord Almighty, his judgement is certain and sure. We will see in Habakkuk chapter 3 that this Lord is the Warrior, the Lord of Hosts, who will fight for his people and who will come in salvation and in judgement.

It reminds us of the question Paul asks in 1 Corinthians 3: what kind of building are you constructing? As believers our lives are secure on the one foundation of Jesus Christ but, Paul says, what materials are you using as you build on that foundation? Are you using those things which are of passing value – 'wood, hay or straw'? Or are you using something that will last for ever – 'gold, silver, (and) costly stones'? How you live your life now matters because, one day, it will be tested. That is not to cast doubt on our future hope; it is simply to underline that the way in which we live our lives does make a difference. Will we look back on our lives and see that we have built with only things which are temporary, or will we have used our time, gifts and talents to have built something that will last for eternity? Will it disappear in a cloud of smoke because it has all been selfish ambition, or will it be lasting, built for eternity?

Notice that each 'woe' that we have looked at so far implies that there is something inbuilt about ungodly behaviour, as if it sows the seeds of its own destruction. In a recent article entitled 'Are you sinning comfortably?', the social commentator Bryan Appleyard tried to update the seven deadly sins. What interested me was his conclusion about justice and judgement. 'The secular minded will shrug their shoulders: it is their favourite gesture. 'So what?' they will say. There is no God to punish us and no hell in which we shall burn. And, unless taken to extremes, none of these sins in themselves is actually criminal. But the point about the 'deadlies' is they're usually their own punishment.'[20]

Appleyard is suggesting that there is something built into these 'deadly sins' which ultimately destroys the person. God is not mocked: we reap what we sow. For Habakkuk, however, it was not simply the inevitable law of retribution. Judgement is certain because of the reality of God's holy character. Although sin inevitably produces its own destructive consequences, the book of Habakkuk reminds us that God's active judgement is also at work – if not immediately, most certainly in the future. It is his world and it is under his control. His judgement will surely punish sin and set things right.

- *What are the things in our lives – perhaps even in our church life – which could easily become a feature of the 'self-aggrandisement' to which this section refers?*
- *The psalmist tells us that 'unless the Lord builds the house, those who build it labour in vain' – what do you think this means in practice?*

● *We referred to Paul's image of 'building with things that will last' (1 Cor. 3:10-15). What does that mean for our value system and ambition?*

● *Sad to say, power can also be abused in the context of Christian community. Spend a while seeking God's forgiveness for when that happens in our own context, and seek his grace to equip us and our church leaders with the meekness of Christ.*

## THE FOURTH WOE: SHAMELESS EXPLOITATION

### Habakkuk 2:15-17

'The violence you have done to Lebanon will overwhelm you and your destruction of animals will terrify you' (2:17). It is interesting that the Lord does not miss this particular element of exploitation of which the Babylonians were guilty: the exploitation of creation, the terrible environmental damage that resulted from Babylonian invasions. In this paragraph we see something of God's concern about the devastation to his creation. Today we speak more and more about 'green theology' and we should not imagine that it is of just marginal interest. God is concerned about the impact of sin in every corner of his creation, including the destruction of forests and cruelty to animals, both of which are mentioned in verse 17. Again the verdict is announced: 'The violence you have done will overwhelm you' (v17).

The other element of exploitation which resonates with us is found in verses 15 and 16, since we identify the activity in our culture too. 'Woe to him who gives drink to his neighbours, pouring it from the wineskin till they are drunk, so that he can gaze on their naked bodies.' This is directed at those who use alcohol to seduce people, something brought to prominence in our day through trials for date rape. But the point of this woe is broader than that. The ungodly have very little respect for the dignity of other people. They will go to any means to achieve their purpose. Other people are simply objects, manipulated and exploited in any way that is necessary. It is glorying in power over others. Whether that is the exploitation of cheap Chinese labourers, or Albanian and Russian women in European brothels, or the exploitation of children in sweatshops, or hostages in Iraq, or the trafficking of refugees – all of these are graphic illustrations of the appalling lack of regard for the dignity of others, the depraved behaviour of those who live their lives without God.

Notice the same pattern in this woe as in all the others. The wicked has brought shame on others (v16) and so now the Lord will bring shame on him. They are chilling words, 'Now it is your turn! Drink and be exposed! The cup from the LORD's right hand is coming . . . and disgrace will cover your glory' (v16).

We can imagine Belshazzar back at the feast. At the beginning of Daniel chapter 5 they are in festive mood, for the Babylonians were renowned for their drunkenness. Then Belshazzar gave orders to bring in the gold and silver goblets that Nebuchadnezzar had taken from the Temple in Jerusalem. And as they drank their wine and praised their gods, that very night the hand of the Sovereign Lord appeared and wrote on the wall. Habakkuk 2:16 was fulfilled. 'Now it's your turn! Drink . . . the cup from the Lord's right hand is coming round to you.'

Clement Freud tells the joke about a wine-waiter who died. His friends stood around the grave and noted the words on the tombstone: 'God finally caught his eye.'

Habakkuk chapter 2 reminds us that God sees what is happening and God acts. The cup of judgement will come. The image of the cup is used by various Old Testament prophets to express the same awful truth. 'The cup filled with the wine of my wrath', records Jeremiah. 'A cup large and deep, it will bring scorn and derision', predicts Ezekiel.

In fact, the words take us to Gethsemane. Jesus, who knew all of these Old Testament passages, takes from his Father the cup of judgement. It is no wonder that initially he shrank from taking it, for the cup represented God's judgement which our sins deserved, but which Jesus was to face at the cross. He drank that cup to the dregs: he bore our sin and took our judgement. His drinking of that cup means that we will never hear God's 'woe' to us. The righteous live by faith in what Jesus has done on the cross in taking that cup of God's judgement. For all true believers, Paul's confident assertion should be written across the woes of Habakkuk chapter 2: 'there is now no condemnation for those who are in Christ Jesus' (Rom. 8:1).

- *The cup of God's wrath has been taken on our behalf by Christ himself. So despite the demands of Habakkuk chapter 2, we read its condemnations this side of Calvary. Spend a while in thanksgiving for the grace and mercy we sinners have experienced through Christ's obedience.*

- *To what extent do you think that our participation in environmental damage brings us under God's judgement?*

- *Exploiting and manipulating others can sometimes be a feature of Christian community, not just the ruthless nations and powerful dictators of our world. Pray for the Lord's help to treat everyone with dignity, respect and true service.*

# THE FIFTH WOE: FOOLISH IDOLATRY

*Habakkuk 2:18-20*

In many ways, this is the culmination of the previous woes. We have looked at the two ways to live and here is the most obvious example of life lived without the true God: it is the folly of worshipping dumb idols. The Babylonians often ascribed their success to their gods and looked for guidance from the idols of their own making. There is a fair amount of satirical mockery in verses 18 and 19, as elsewhere in the Old Testament descriptions of idolatry, and its purpose is to demonstrate the difference between the powerless non-entities of the pagan nations and Israel's living all-powerful, all-controlling God. 'For those who make them trust in their own creations; they make idols that cannot speak . . . Can it give guidance?' (v18).

We may think this is merely pagan religion, distant from contemporary western culture, but it is very typical of our society as well. People long for guidance, hoping to make sense of their lives and gain some sense of control. So they turn to astrology or ouija boards or to new age superstitions. G.K. Chesterton was quite right when he said, 'When people stop believing in the truth, they don't believe in nothing, they believe in anything.' Contemporary idolatry is all around us. Every generation seeks substitute deities. Perhaps most obviously in our culture, the main idol is the self. The social commentator Bryan Appleyard suggests, 'The only possible sin today is the sin against oneself. The idea is everywhere – self-help, self-esteem, making the best of oneself, looking one's best and self-realisation are the great contemporary virtues. Therefore the one recognised sin is failure to look after *numero uno*.'[21]

Do you know the joke, 'What's the difference between God and a lawyer'? Answer: God doesn't think he's a lawyer. But we shouldn't be too tough on the lawyers, for the attitude is true of us all. We think we're in charge. We have become the centre of our little universe. And whatever the substitute god might be – possessions, plans, or self-obsession – God pronounces his woe upon all who trust in the things of their own creation. Notice verse 18, 'Of what value is an idol, since a man has carved it? Or an image that teaches lies?' It's an intriguing suggestion – an idol that lies. It is counterfeit. The idols in people's lives are self-deceiving, blinding people to their own helplessness. The supposed worship of an idol deceives them about their guilt and their need of forgiveness. They are ignorant of the fact that they depend on God himself for every breath they take.

● *We have suggested that idolatry is alive and well in our own culture, particularly with the emphasis on 'the self.' What are the ways in which this might demonstrate itself in our church or Christian life?*

---

**FURTHER STUDY**
In this chapter we have seen that sinfulness not only harbours the seeds of its own destruction but also calls forth God's righteous judgement. This theme is clear in the New Testament too, and it is significant in relation to our understanding of the Christian gospel, particularly the saving work of Christ. Read the following passages, noting the language of judgement but also the promise of deliverance.

Romans 1:18 – 2:5; Ephesians 5:5,6; Colossians 3:5,6;
1 Thessalonians 5:1-3; 2 Peter 3:3-13.

**REFLECTION AND RESPONSE**
A chapter of this kind impacts at several levels. We might well feel a sense of despair about the extent of sin in our world, of which these

five sections are powerful illustrations. But we must remember what we have seen already: the facts of God's sovereign control, his faithful promises and his ultimate justice. Spend a while praying about the international situations known to you or fellow members of your church – the countries where exploitation and trafficking of people is rife; where the excesses of capitalism and materialism take their toll; where dictators oppress their populations; where Christians are persecuted. Let us join our intercession with thanksgiving that none of this is lost on the all-seeing Lord whose purposes will be finally achieved.

# CHAPTER 6

# The certainty of God's rule

Aim: to rejoice in the fact that, both now and in the future, God's rule is certain and his ultimate glory is assured.

**FOCUS ON THE THEME**
In the midst of the darkness of chapter 2, with its resounding Woes, there shine two verses which declare the great certainties of the Lord's sovereignty. These affirmations are all the more significant because of their context, and they represent the answer to Habakkuk's bewildered complaints.

*Read: Habakkuk 2:6-20*
*Key verses: Habakkuk 2:14,20*

**Outline**

*The certainty of God's rule*
A present reality
A future certainty

In the final woe we noted the contrast between the helpless and dumb idols and the sovereignty of the Almighty Lord. Unlike the idols, he is never unable to see, hear, speak or act. He is the Lord of heaven and earth. And this brings us to another certainty which shines through in chapter 2.

Amidst the ringing declarations of woe, with their message of the certainty of judgement, there are two wonderful certainties declared, one present and one future.

## A PRESENT REALITY (2:20)

As we have seen, the context is one where the idols are declared to be dumb – silent. But now the word comes, 'The LORD is in his holy temple, let all the earth be silent before him' (v20). It is onomatopoeic in Hebrew, like our word 'Hush': be silent, stop all the arguments, all the arrogant assertions of human power, the pretensions of human glory, the petty ambitions. It is a call for reverence, because the one who is speaking is the Lord of the universe. He is the Sovereign Lord, active in history; he calls all men and women, all nations and governments to bow the knee to him.

In these few words we have the answer to Habakkuk's complaint. Why isn't God acting in the way Habakkuk thought he should? The answer is stated in a simple assertion. The Lord is seated on his kingly throne, in the place of ultimate authority, above heaven and earth, high above his creatures. Before him there is no room for asserting our independence. Instead, we are called to humble submission to the Lord of the universe. And unlike the impotent deities of paganism, here is the God who is in control, who can be relied upon. Here is the absolute certainty, for this God is the unchanging Ruler of the universe, which he created and sustains and which ultimately he will wrap up and bring to completion. The people in Habakkuk's day were foolish to turn to the substitute 'godlets', whether idols, magic or black arts, for they were called into relationship with the Sovereign Lord.

The simplicity of verse 20 speaks clearly in the fractured world of our day too. The more we grow in our

understanding of the majesty of the God whom we worship
– the God who calls us into fellowship with himself and
who cares for his children – the more we will learn to
entrust the uncertainties of our lives to his good purposes.

● *Why does the fact that 'the Lord is in his temple' provoke the
call that the world should be 'silent before him'?*

● *How would you reply to someone who suggests that, given
the terrors of our world, the Christian belief in the Lord's
rule is simply whistling in the dark to keep our spirits up?*

## A FUTURE CERTAINTY (2:14)

'For the earth will be filled with knowledge of the glory of
the LORD, as the waters cover the sea' (v14). What an
incredible shaft of light in the darkness. In the context of
the power of empires and the pretensions of human rulers,
the Lord speaks of the certainty of what will be left on that
final day: the universal knowledge of the glory of God.
Similar words are used by Isaiah too: 'They will neither
harm nor destroy on all my holy mountain, for the earth
will be full of the knowledge of the LORD as the waters
cover the sea' (Is. 11:9). The earlier part of Isaiah 11 refers to
a shoot which will come up from the stump of Jesse. It is a
prophecy of great David's Greater Son, pointing towards
the ultimate victory of the Lord Jesus, to the completion of
his purposes in the destruction of evil and the
establishment of a new heaven and earth, the home of
righteousness.

Intriguingly, Habakkuk adds to the words of Isaiah – he
includes the word 'glory.' 'The earth will be filled with the
knowledge of the glory of the Lord.' Why is that? Perhaps
because the word glory encompasses the ultimate goal of
all human history. If we are uncertain about what is

happening in our world, we should remember that this is where everything is heading. The ultimate truth, the final word, the enduring reality, will be the glory of the Lord. And all other human glories, such as those which were described and mocked in the woes of chapter 2, will fade away in the light of that supreme glory, his royal majesty. It is a wonderful description of the ultimate triumph of God.

> Jesus shall reign where'er the sun
> doth his successive journeys run.
> His kingdom stretch from shore to shore
> 'til moons shall wax and wane no more.[22]

This is not only a great encouragement to Christians who wonder where the world is heading but it is a great incentive to us to tell others the good news of the gospel. As Psalm 96 encourages us, 'Declare his glory among the nations.' That is both an act of worship and an act of mission, for in both we are motivated by that same longing – to declare his glory. Our task is to call our friends, our neighbours, our work colleagues, our fellow students, all people – to worship him. As John Piper expressed it, 'mission exists because worship doesn't.'

David Bryant defines a world Christian in this way.

> A world Christian is someone who is so gripped by the glory of God and the glory of his global purpose, that he chooses to align himself with God's mission to fill the earth with the knowledge of his glory as the waters cover the sea. The burning prayer of the world Christian is, "Let the peoples praise thee O God, let all the peoples praise thee" (Ps. 96:3).[23]

The last word will not belong to earth's kingdoms. Habakkuk gives us a very different perspective on who is in control. It will be a glorious world filled with the awareness of God's purposes, of God's presence and of God's glory.

On the Sunday after the atrocities of 9/11, we sang a wonderful hymn in our church in Oxford: 'All my hope on God is founded.' It contains a very appropriate verse after the world had witnessed the destruction in Manhattan.

Pride of man and earthly glory,
sword and crown betray his trust;
with what care and toil he buildeth,
tower and temple fall to dust.
But God's power, hour by hour,
is my temple and my tower.[24]

This verse, Habakkuk 2:14, is the reason why Habakkuk could go on trusting God in a world of darkness and uncertainty. And so can we, because the reality of verse 14 has been secured through the work of Jesus Christ. All our hope on God is founded. Of course, we await its final completion – a theme which we have met already and will do so again in chapter 3 – but this is the promise, this is the hope in which our faith in God is founded.

These are the great certainties in an uncertain world. We live our lives now in the light of the twin truths of this chapter: the certainty of God's judgement and the certainty of God's glorious rule. In the New Testament it finds its focus in a wonderful doxology: 'Therefore, God exalted him to the highest place and gave him the name which is above every name, that at the name of Jesus every knee should bow, in heaven and on earth and under the earth and every tongue confess that Jesus Christ is Lord, to the glory of God the Father' (Phil. 2:9-11).

# REVIEW OF SECTION 3

The dramatic woes of chapter 2 are part of the journey which Habakkuk is taking, and it is worth pausing to note the progression of the prophecy so far. From his sustained questions and bewilderment as he reflected on the violence and injustice of his day, and the Lord's word that worse was to come, Habakkuk had climbed the walls of the city and, in hearing the word of the Lord through patient listening, had gained a new perspective on what was happening in his world. Far from events careering out of control, God would act in judgement – first on his own people, then on the Babylonians, and then outwards and onwards through human history.

Habakkuk is learning that God's rule is certain and God's glory will be the eventual outcome, whatever present circumstances might suggest. But how is God going to bring about the longed-for deliverance and salvation for which Habakkuk has been appealing? We turn to the final chapter of the prophecy to continue the journey from 'Why to Worship.'

---

### FURTHER STUDY
There are several Bible passages which point to these future certainties and which fill out Habakkuk's vision. Spend some time reading them through, capturing in the poetic and prophetic language of each passage the heart-warming and spine-strengthening realities to which they point.

Isaiah 11:1-11; Ezekiel 34:25-31; Ephesians 1:9-12; Revelation 21:1-8

### REFLECTION AND RESPONSE
We have suggested that both worship and mission are motivated by a desire to declare God's glory. In today's Christianity, there seems to

be much more emphasis on worship than on mission: why do you think that might be?

There is no doubt that Habakkuk's vision of the earth filled with the knowledge of the glory of the Lord is profoundly moving. But why do we reflect on this so rarely? In what ways can we keep this vision more prominent in our hearts and minds and in our Christian community?

# Watch!

## Habakkuk 3:1-15

# Watch!

HABAKKUK 3:1-15

## INTRODUCTION

Some years ago I had my one and only experience of abseiling, a sport that involves being dropped over a cliff backwards. After you have roped up, the person at the top belays the rope, letting you down at the speed of your choosing. You have to trust the rope but you must also trust the person at the top. Because he was a good friend, I knew he wouldn't let me down! As in so many situations of life, trust grows out of our knowledge of the person.

The story of Habakkuk has confronted us with one major question: can we trust God's purposes for our life, our future, our nation, our world? Ultimately it all depends on our view of God. In the 1960s, the American writer, A.W. Tozer, called the evangelical church to face the critical need of revival in the face of decline. How could this be achieved? Tozer wrote

> The answer might easily disappoint some persons, for it is anything but profound. I bring no esoteric cryptogram, no mystic code to be painfully deciphered, I appeal to no hidden law of the unconscious, no occult knowledge meant only for the few. The secret is an open one which the wayfaring man may read. It is simply the old and ever-new counsel: Acquaint thyself with God. To regain her lost power the church must see heaven opened and have a transforming vision of God.

As we open Habakkuk chapter 3, we have that opportunity.

How can we possibly understand the infinite, majestic God? Mark Buchanan recounts the story of St Augustine, who one day was walking along the seashore, reflecting on the question of the majesty of God, when he saw a small boy. The boy had dug a hole in the sand. He had a large shell and he ran down to the sea, filling the shell with seawater and then returned and poured the seawater into the hole. Augustine asked him what was he doing and the boy replied, 'I'm going to pour the sea into that hole'. At that point, Augustine realised what he had been trying to do: standing at the edge of the ocean of God's greatness and trying to grasp it with his finite mind. It's an almost preposterous idea: to attempt to understand the manifestation of God's greatness and glory.[25]

We long for a deeper understanding and experience of God. We are hungry for that reality. Don Carson has expressed it like this

> The one thing we most urgently need in Western
> Christendom is a deeper knowledge of God. We need to
> know God better. When it comes to knowing God we are a
> culture of the spiritually stunted. So much of our religion is
> packaged to address our felt needs – and these are almost
> uniformly anchored in our pursuit of our own happiness
> and fulfilment. We are not captivated by his holiness and
> love; his thoughts and words capture too little of our
> imagination, too little of our discourse, too few of our
> priorities.[26]

Habakkuk's journey is nearly over. But before his closing doxology he is called to open his eyes to a remarkable, transforming vision of God. It is a vision of God's character and a vision of his actions, past, present and future. So the fourth word in Habakkuk's journey is 'Watch'!

● *We quoted A.W. Tozer: 'To regain her lost power the church must see heaven opened and have a transforming vision of God.' As we begin this section, spend a moment in prayer that these familiar themes – the call to know God more profoundly – will not be superficially acknowledged but deeply rooted in our lives and churches.*

# CHAPTER 7

# Habakkuk's appeal

*Aim: to understand what it means to pray 'your will be done'.*

**FOCUS ON THE THEME**
So far in Habakkuk's prophecy we have seen the dialogue between the bewildered man of faith and the Lord Almighty. It has moved from complaint, to answer, from complaint, to answer. That final answer, expounding the certainty of God's judgement and rule, leads Habakkuk to pray for God's purposes to be achieved. In the opening two verses of chapter 3, he demonstrates how such a prayer should be framed.

*Read: Habakkuk 3:1,2*

### Outline

*Habakkuk's appeal*
A conviction about God's work
A call for God's action
A cry for God's mercy

Although the chapter is introduced as a prayer, it is also a song and there are several clues through the chapter. *Selah* (vs 3,9,13) is a term possibly designating a musical break; at the close of the chapter there is a musical instruction (v19); and in verse 1 there is a rather unusual word, *shigionoth*, probably an instruction about tempo which implies a strong rhythm. This particular song was no funeral dirge. Given its extraordinarily dramatic descriptions and dynamic pace, it was certainly *up-tempo*. When we read it, we can almost hear the brass section, the drums, the driving rhythm of the bass! So after all we have looked at, all of the struggles, challenges and turmoil which Habakkuk had faced, what does he do? He starts to sing – and he encourages others to start singing too.

One way in which God's people keep going when they are facing challenges of all kinds is to sing about what God has done. On my travels I meet it in country after country, and it is deeply moving to see God's people caught up in singing about what God has done. So many Christians are surrounded by pressures, mocked and opposed by enemies, deprived of normal human privileges – and yet they sing. And why? Because singing captures our hearts and our emotions as well as our minds. It has been well said that this is the reason why the longest book in the Bible is a songbook.

● *Francis Schaeffer, commenting on Romans 1:21, once said that the first sign of our rebellion against God is a lack of a thankful heart. Do you think that is true?*

The whole chapter represents one of the model prayers from which we can learn so much. Let's look at three things about Habakkuk's appeal.

## A CONVICTION ABOUT GOD'S WORK (3:2)

'Lord, I have heard of your fame; I stand in awe of your deeds O LORD' (v2). We can sense immediately the change of tone from the anxious prayers and appeals of chapter 1. Here there is a sense of humble commitment. He is no longer arguing, for he recognises that everything that God has said and done is just. Calvin translates the verse 'I heard Thy voice.' Standing there on the walls above Jerusalem, Habakkuk had heard God's word, the report of God's work, both in the past and in the prophecies of what was to come. He stands in awe, probably alarmed, with a sense of submission and godly fear.

We will see this stated even more starkly when we come to verse 16. But by this point in the prophecy Habakkuk has recognised that God is in control of the situation. He is ready to accept the just purposes of God. It is a kind of 'Amen' to what God had been saying to him. It was his humble response – 'yes, Lord, now I understand. It is your work'.

● *One of the temptations in Christian service is to imagine that it is our work. But Paul was at pains to underline a different reality. Take a look at Philippians 1:6 and 2:13 and discuss what these verses might mean for our understanding of God's work.*

## A CALL FOR GOD'S ACTION (3:2)

'Renew them in our day, in our time make them known' (v2). Secondly, Habakkuk longs that God's powerful work in the past should be seen in his own day, so that the people of God would know that he is in control of their lives and of history. Chapter 3 has many references to the story of the Exodus, celebrated frequently by the psalmists and the prophets as their finest hour. And so he appeals, 'Please Lord, repeat that kind of redemption. Renew your work now just as you did in the past'. It is a call for God's action. He wants to see the work of God in the past renewed now, not just in some distant future. And he is clear about what matters: renew *your* work. He wants God's purposes fulfilled, God's work established in his day. It is a prayer with which we are familiar – 'Your Kingdom come, your will be done.'

As I read these verses, I can't help thinking about what dominates my praying. Is this the kind of prayer that I pray? Am I longing for God's purposes to be fulfilled, for the church to be renewed? Christians in Europe live in a continent where, by and large, the church is not growing. The majority of God's people today are found in the southern hemisphere, and one reason for the shift in the centre of gravity is undoubtedly the extraordinary gospel passion and committed prayer of God's people in these countries. I have a friend who lives and works in the majority world. He wonders if there is some relation between the suffering, poverty and daily challenge of living in some of these countries, and the extraordinary sense of dependence which Christians express – and therefore the blessing of God which they enjoy. There is surely a correlation between those things: dependent prayer and God's blessing.

When Habakkuk appeals, 'In our day, in our time', perhaps he means 'even in the midst of judgement, Lord, come in deliverance'. Although in a moment we will stress the importance of calling to mind what God has done in the past, Habakkuk does not want an experience which is just hearsay or second-hand. Rather, he appeals that they would experience God's saving presence now, just as they did in the past.

- *There are some groups who urge us to pray for revival. Why do we not respond to that call more energetically?*
- *Discuss in the group what dominates our praying. Our prayers tend to go out in concentric circles, with ourselves and our personal or family needs at the centre. But what priorities do you think would shape our prayers if we were to pray like Habakkuk in verse 2?*

## A CRY FOR GOD'S MERCY (3:2)

We can identify the longings of his aching heart in the third element of his prayer, expressed in verse 3: 'In wrath remember mercy.' It is an understandable cry. He had heard of God's judgement on his own people in Judah, the fearful reality of God's anger against sin, and so he prays that, alongside God's wrath, he would remember mercy. Once again, his prayer is a model to us. The essence of prayer is 'to plead God's character in God's presence.' Remember mercy, Lord. Be true to your character.

You may have noticed several references in this chapter to God's wrath, and the verses make for uncomfortable reading. Some Christians today hesitate to ascribe such emotions to God. Isn't wrath a figment of the imagination of those preachers who like to adopt the role of an austere prophet? We might be disturbed to discover that, in the Old Testament alone, there are over twenty words for God's wrath and anger, and apparently over 580 references to him acting in that way.

If we stand back for a moment, we can see why his wrath is essential to our understanding of God. How can God be God if he does not reveal his wrath 'against all the godlessness and wickedness of men' (Rom. 1:18)? Paradoxically, it is because of God's wrath against wickedness that we have the comfort of knowing that his justice will be fulfilled, that the day of restoration will finally come.

Mark Meynell, writing on the subject of the cross, quotes the true story of the nail bombings which occurred in London some years ago. The nail bomber was targeting particular minority groups: one bomb went off in Brixton, one in Brick Lane and then a third bomb exploded in a gay pub in Soho. A day later a young man was captured by the police. His name was David Copeland and he was charged with the bombings. His father made a press statement in which he said that he and his family totally condemned the barbaric bombings. 'If David is guilty of these awful acts of violence then we also totally condemn him for carrying out those acts.'[27] To condemn their son did not deny their love for him, nor would it be inconsistent to call for such a crime to be punished. The call for wrongs to be righted can co-exist with deep love and compassion.

I know I am not the only one who identifies with Habakkuk's cry, 'Lord, in wrath remember mercy.' We know what we deserve. I saw a cartoon not long ago, with a husband and wife standing in a queue before the gates of heaven. Waiting for their turn to face judgement, the wife whispered to her husband 'Now, Harold, whatever you do, please don't demand what's coming to you.' We are all too aware of what our rebellion deserves. But wrath and mercy are found together right at the heart of the Christian gospel.

It is important to hold these two truths together, for sometimes Christians tend to polarise, emphasising one truth over another. More commonly, in our desire to make the Christian message acceptable, we might be tempted to suggest that, in today's culture, we should emphasise God's love and play down the idea of God's wrath. But these two qualities always belong together, and the Bible frequently describes this duality within God. John Stott's classic book, *The Cross of Christ*[28] helpfully explains this duality. Here are a few examples which he gives. In Exodus 34 God is described as 'the compassionate and gracious God . . . Yet he does not leave the guilty unpunished.' Or Isaiah refers to him as 'a righteous God and a Saviour.' Paul reminds us of the 'kindness and the sternness of God' and John describes the Lord as 'faithful and just,' the one who will both act righteously and also forgive sinners like us.

In each of these ways we see that his wrath and love belong together as two dynamic concepts which are complementary both in God's nature and his actions. In our praying, we know how important it is to take the words of Habakkuk's prayer and to appeal for God's mercy on the grounds of Christ's work. Whatever Habakkuk teaches us about the inevitability of judgement and God's wrath, it also points us to the Lord who shows mercy, the Lord who will redeem his people.

- *What kind of distorted impressions of God do people in your workplace or neighbourhood have?*
- *Why do we find it hard to hold together in our minds both God's wrath and God's love?*
- *In what ways does an understanding of the cross help us to understand God's character?*
- *If you are explaining the gospel to someone who is not a Christian, would you talk about the goodness of God or the severity of God? Or would you tackle both? Can you think of examples from the way Jesus approached people, or the way the early Christians preached in Acts, which give clues to how this should be done?*

---

### FURTHER STUDY

Here are some of the passages cited by John Stott in *The Cross of Christ* which point to the duality to which we have referred. Look them up and read them in their context, noting the significance of the descriptions of God's nature and actions.

Exodus 34:6,7; Isaiah 45:21,22; Romans 11:22; 1 John 1:8,9.

### REFLECTION AND RESPONSE

We have looked at three elements that should shape our prayers: a conviction about God's work; a call for God's action; a cry for God's mercy. Perhaps it would be useful to use this simple frame for a time of prayer, ideally with others in the group. If, like Habakkuk, we are overwhelmed by the sinfulness of our society and of our own hearts, spend some time making that same appeal to the Lord: 'in wrath, remember mercy.'

# CHAPTER 8

# Habakkuk's vision

*Aim: to become more fully aware of the greatness of the God who saves.*

**FOCUS ON THE THEME**
Habakkuk has prayed for God's work of salvation and now he is given a remarkable vision of the coming of the Lord. Its dimensions are breathtaking, its descriptions are dramatic, its impact is overwhelming. The Lord is coming in victory – then, now and in the future.

*Read: Habakkuk 3:3-15*
*Key verse: Habakkuk 3:13*

**Outline**

*Habakkuk's vision*
The coming of the Lord
The power of the Lord
The victory of the Lord

Habakkuk's vision is a profound revelation of God's nature and work, on a par with the great visions of Scripture. It reminds us of the story of Job, who confronted similar challenges to Habakkuk, specially in his personal and family life. As a man of integrity he too had many questions. But it has been well said: Job asks 'Why?' and God answers 'Who.' God's reply is not a detailed argument but an extraordinary panorama of his powerful work and his profound wisdom. Job is not given neat solutions but an overwhelming vision of God. Like Habakkuk, he is told to watch.

Throughout Scripture the coming of the Lord to individuals and to his people was evident in a variety of unexpected ways. 'A burning bush, a ladder of angels, a still small voice, a wheel in a wheel, a lofty throne, a solar eclipse, a sheet filled with animals, a trumpet sound – all announce the coming of the Lord.'

This is exactly what Habakkuk encounters. The vision swept him off his feet. He was sent reeling by the remarkable vision of the warrior God outlined in these verses. His reactions are described either side of the vision: 'I have heard of your fame, I stand in awe of your deeds' (v2); 'I heard and my heart pounded, my lips quivered at the sound; decay crept into my bones and my legs trembled' (v16).

The vision has a number of important references to what God has done in the past. He retraces the route taken by the Israelites in the Exodus, when God delivered his people. Remembering God's acts in the past is basic to Old Testament prayer and is very important for us too. When we are bewildered about our own world, we are called to remember what God has done in the past.

The call to remember is frequently heard in the Old Testament. Recalling what God had done in the past was an incentive to live life now with gratitude and trust. God's people were encouraged to keep rehearsing the stories of the great saving events in their history. Why? Because they were reminders of God's grace. They reinforced the reality of God's love for his people. If you asked God's people in the Old Testament, 'How do you know God loves you?', their reply would be, 'Look at what God has done for us. He rescued us from Egypt, he cared for us in the wilderness, he defeated our enemies.' These were the great historical realities on which their faith was founded, the objective core of their faith. 'Remember you were once slaves; remember how the Lord rescued you.' This momentous story was proof of God's unfailing love for them.

And for Christians, the manoeuvre is exactly the same. Our faith is founded on events which have already happened, on facts in history where God has acted decisively. As Paul said to the Corinthians, remember the things of 'first importance' – Christ died, Christ was buried, Christ rose (1 Cor. 15:3,4); and as he said to Timothy, 'Remember Jesus Christ, raised from the dead' (2 Tim. 2:8).

When we are tempted to think that God must have forgotten about us or that God doesn't really care, as Habakkuk might have done, then we look at the cross and the resurrection. Our faith is not founded on nice religious ideas. As Chris Wright has commented, 'The gospel is not just a good idea, it is good news.' It is founded on what God has done.

- *What does 'looking back' mean for Christians? Where do we look and how is that an encouragement to our life of faith?*
- *Earlier we commented on the value of committing key Bible passages to memory. Why not agree with your group to try and do that on a regular basis?*

The vision in Habakkuk 3 includes these backward glances; but Habakkuk also looks at the present in the light of the future. In fact, the Jewish mind didn't neatly categorise into past, present and future, and so we find in these verses a kaleidoscope of references, sometimes looking back, sometimes looking forward. God rescued his people in the past; God will come again to rescue them in the future. We will see these dimensions as we highlight three features of the vision.

## THE COMING OF THE LORD (3:3-5)

The vision begins by proclaiming that God is on the move. As he comes nearer and nearer, the impact of his glorious presence becomes more and more dramatic. 'God came from Teman, the Holy One from Mount Paran' (v3). This is a reference to the area of Sinai where God first revealed himself to Moses at the burning bush and where subsequently, in a dramatic revelation of his power and presence, he revealed the law to his people.

Verses 3 and 4 describe the radiance of his presence as he comes. 'His glory covered the heavens and his praise filled the earth. His splendour was like the sunrise; rays flashed from his hand, where his power was hidden.' The verses conjure up the images of fire and cloud that characterised that Mount Sinai encounter, reminding Habakkuk and all singers of this song of the glory and power of God whenever he comes to his people. Just as at Sinai, his coming is accompanied by a radiance that is overwhelming and awe-inspiring. Habakkuk sees it here illuminating the entire world.

In *The Message*, Eugene Peterson paraphrases it like this, 'Skies are blazing with his splendour, his praises sounding through the earth. His cloud-brightness like dawn, exploding, spreading, forked-lightning shooting from his hand – what power hidden in that fist!' Such is the drama and colour of this remarkable vision of the coming of God. Then in his coming in the Exodus he was accompanied by extraordinary signs, described in verse 5: 'plague went before; pestilence followed in his steps.' The Egyptians, powerful though they were, were terrified by that coming of the Lord.

Habakkuk remembers those great events of the past but, as throughout the song, there is also an anticipation of God's future intervention. His coming will always be a source of hope for God's people. As we saw from Hebrews 10, the writer to the Hebrews quotes from Habakkuk chapter 2:3, making application to the coming of the Lord. 'Do not throw away your confidence; it will be richly rewarded. You need to persevere ... For in just a very little while, (here he quotes Habakkuk) "He who is coming will come and will not delay"' (Heb. 10:36,37). The glorious manifestation of God's coming described in Habakkuk 3:3-4, witnessed by the entire universe, also anticipates that day when we will see Jesus coming. Matthew describes similar dramatic manifestations accompanying that arrival: 'For as lightning that comes from the east is visible even in the west, so will be the coming of the Son of Man . . . They will see the Son of Man coming on the clouds of the sky, with power and great glory' (Mt. 24:27,30).

This is where Habakkuk's vision is pointing us: to that ultimate day. In essence, God is saying, 'Watch, I am coming.' It will be a day of judgement and of deliverance, a day of wrath and of mercy, a day when human history will be finally wrapped up. We are to 'look for the glorious appearing of our great God and Saviour, Jesus Christ'.

Lord Shaftesbury, the great social reformer who was totally committed to the needs of this world, also had another horizon. Near the end of his life he said, 'I do not think that in the last forty years I have lived one conscious hour that was not influenced by the thought of the Lord's return.'

- *In what ways does the thought of Christ's return impact your life?*
- *If you knew Christ was returning in one month's time, what changes would you make to the way you live your life?*

## THE POWER OF THE LORD (3:6,7)

Just as there were great convulsions at Sinai when God came to his people, so his power is demonstrated whenever he comes in salvation and deliverance. The poetry of verse 6 demonstrates the almost cosmic implications of his arrival: 'He stood and shook the earth; he looked and made the nations tremble; the ancient mountains crumbled, the age-old hills collapsed.' He is the Creator and at his coming even the mountains crumble before him. The eternal hills bow before the splendour of this eternal God. Cushan and Midian (v7) were nations which bordered Egypt, so they would have seen the great deliverance that God brought about for his people and would have trembled with distress and anguish (v7). In Habakkuk's vision no nation will be exempt from his power and his judgement.

The prophet Isaiah uses very similar language. Writing to those in his own day who were tempted to believe that God had given up on his people, he expands their vision: 'Who has measured the waters in the hollow of his hand? . . . Who has held the dust of the earth in a basket, or weighed the mountains on the scales? He sits enthroned above the circle of the earth, and its people are like grasshoppers' (Is. 40:12,22). As Jim Packer has expressed it: 'The world dwarfs us all but God dwarfs the world. All the feverish activity of its six billion does no more to affect him than the chirping and jumping of grasshoppers in the summer sun does to affect us.'[29]

The early Christians began their prayer in Acts 4: 'Sovereign Lord . . . you made the heaven and the earth.' Their appeal was based on the fact that the powerful Lord of creation was in control of the forces ranged against them. And so it is for God's people now. The centre of power today is not London, Washington, or Moscow: it is the Lord God Omnipotent.

Many of the descriptive images in Habakkuk 3 are picked up in the New Testament. Peter describes the cataclysmic events of the end times

> The heavens will disappear with a roar; the elements will be destroyed by fire and the earth and everything in it will be laid bare . . . That day will bring about the destruction of the heavens by fire and the elements will melt in the heat. But in keeping with his promise, we are looking forward to a new heaven and a new earth, the home of righteousness (2 Pet. 3:10,12).

Peter is making it abundantly clear to the people of his day, just as Habakkuk did, that this *will* happen. God is in control of this world. As Habakkuk says at the end of verse 6: 'His ways are eternal.' We are reminded once again: he is in control.

In David Atkinson's commentary on the book of Job, he recounts the story of a pastor making his way back home during the Second World War, after a night of comforting people in the London blitz. He meets a fellow pastor who had been doing the same thing but who was bewildered and exasperated as he sought to care for broken people. He explained, 'I wish I was on the throne of the universe for just ten minutes.' His colleague replied, 'If you were on the throne for ten minutes, I would not wish to live in your universe for ten seconds.'[30]

In chapter 3 Habakkuk is describing the powerful Lord of the universe, the One who is eternal. He is the Sovereign Lord, in control of creation, history and all of the nations. No wonder they will tremble at his coming! And in these two themes – the coming of the Lord and the power of the Lord – we find the foundation for security and comfort which we need so much in hard-pressed situations.

● *Discuss together those manifestations of God's power on which you meditate most of all. His work in creation? In the*

*story of deliverance in Exodus? His healing power? His*
*power experienced in weakness? How do these different*
*expressions of God's power at work encourage you in your*
*praying and in your response to the challenges of Christian*
*discipleship?*

## THE VICTORY OF THE LORD (VS 8-15)

This final section introduces a number of images associated
with the Red Sea deliverance. In the dramatic poetry of the
song, the Lord uses the elements of his creation in his
judgement. Look at verse 8: 'Were you angry with the rivers,
O LORD? Was your wrath against the streams? Did you rage
against the sea when you rode with your horses and your
victorious chariots?' God demonstrated his power in these
elements; he was the general leading his forces to victory.

In verse 11 there is the image of creation itself standing still
at that moment, possibly a reference to the story in Joshua
10, where the sun remained still in order to allow Joshua to
win the battle. In verses 12 and 13 there is a description of
the one who destroys the enemy: 'In wrath you strode
through the earth and in anger you threshed the nations'
(v12). 'You crushed the leader of the land of wickedness, you
stripped him from head to feet' (v13). In verse 15 there is an
allusion to the Red Sea deliverance and God's power over
the fearsome chaos of the sea. 'You trampled the sea with
your horses, churning the great waters.'

You can't miss the force of the poetry, as he tramples the
enemy under his feet, crushes the head of the wicked and
destroys the enemy. And the battle is fought for one clear
purpose. Although there are descriptions of judgement,
there are also significant references to salvation. Notice in
verse 8 that God is riding upon his chariot of victory. The
word used for 'victory' is actually 'salvation.' The Greek

version of the Old Testament renders it: 'Your chariot which is salvation.' It is God coming to save, and here we see the focal point of this remarkable vision.

Do you remember Habakkuk's first prayer: 'How long . . . must I cry for help, but you do not listen?' (Hab. 1:2). Here in chapter 3 Habakkuk's vision is the proof that God hears and that God acts, for this is an account of God's deliverance of his people. It was the very thing that Habakkuk was crying out for, the assurance he needed that God keeps his promises, he remembers his covenant.

The purpose of God's coming is the salvation of his people. And that is reinforced in verse 13: 'You came out to deliver your people, to save your anointed one.' What God did in the Exodus deliverance he will do again. He will rescue his people and he will bring them home. That was fulfilled for some of God's people after the immediate judgement that Habakkuk and Jeremiah had predicted, for after the exile some finally returned home. God had delivered his people, bringing them back to Jerusalem. But these verses also anticipate the deliverance of God's people in the future as well. There is a significant reference in verse 13: 'to save your anointed one.' The anointed is the Messiah, translated in the Greek as 'Christ.' The word 'anointed' was sometimes used of the kings of Israel, even of a pagan king, Cyrus, who was used by God to deliver his people. But the word also points to the true Messiah, Jesus, the Christ. At the cross, the Lord Jesus was our substitute in bearing God's righteous anger. It was there that wrath and mercy met. God raised Jesus to life – or to use the language of verse 13 – 'saved his anointed.' So Jesus won the decisive battle over human sin, over all of the cosmic hosts of wickedness.

In his letter to the Colossians Paul uses graphic language when he talks about Christ's victory. 'And having disarmed the powers and authorities, he made a public spectacle of them, triumphing over them by the cross' (Col. 2:15). Many people, Christian and non-Christian alike, are all too aware of the reality of evil and of dark forces. And Jesus' mission was to free us from Satan's oppression, to liberate us from the kingdom of darkness, neatly summed up in John's purpose statement: 'The reason the Son of God appeared was to destroy the devil's work' (1 Jn. 3:8).

The language of Habakkuk 3 describes the victory of the Lord, crushing the leader of the land of wickedness. 'You stripped him from head to foot' (v13). It is almost as if Paul had this in mind as he describes the dimensions of Christ's work on the cross. 'Having disarmed the powers and authorities, he made a public spectacle of them, triumphing over them by the cross' (Col. 2:15). The NIV uses the picture of evil spirit powers, terrorists from hell being stripped of their weapons. So the cross was the place of that unmasking, the disarming of every power which stands against God and against his people. Now through his death and resurrection he has freed us from the fear of evil and delivered us from every demonic force. What Habakkuk described in his overwhelming vision was finally fulfilled in Christ: the victory of the Lord.

## REVIEW OF SECTION 4

Habakkuk's vision portrays these three realities: the coming of the Lord, the power of the Lord and and the victory of the Lord. They each point to that ultimate reality of Jesus' own victory. Earlier we saw that there is often a point of tension between what we believe and what's going on in our world. All we have said about the victory of Christ on the cross, and the overcoming of every cosmic power of evil, might evoke the response that such theology doesn't match with our experience. And it is true. Satan has been defeated but has not yet been finally eliminated. It is often rightly said that we live our lives in the overlap between the now and the not yet, experiencing the tension between what we believe and what is happening around us. We live in a world where the influence of evil is still very evident.

I find it helpful to think of this particular illustration. Imagine that you recorded a video of a football game, say, between Oxford and Everton, and Oxford scrapes by, 5-1. Your team wins! And now you are watching the video replay. But as you watch, you see Everton move forward. They're very fast, moving the ball out to the wings and pressing towards the goal. You begin to wonder – they might win this game. But then you remember, No, the game's already won. You know the outcome.

We Christians already know the result. In our struggles we still face the hostility of Satanic forces, we still feel the pull of sin and often witness the advance of evil. But we can be absolutely sure that Jesus has secured the victory. This is a vital perspective in our own Christian walk. In Habakkuk's day there were many reasons to be tempted to think that God's people were losing ground and that evil was triumphing. And there are all kinds of reasons why we Christians also feel much the same, imagining that we might not finally make it to our home in heaven. So we must remember this truth: the events of Christ's death and resurrection have already taken place and, precisely because of this, the outcome is already sure. As he reeled at the overwhelming vision, Habakkuk knew that this God could be trusted with his life, with his future and even with the destiny of the international powers. God was in control.

Looking back to the victory of the cross and looking forward to its ultimate fulfillment in the coming of Jesus Christ, let's live our lives now fully and freely in the service of Christ our Redeemer.

**REFLECTION AND RESPONSE**

- The image of the victory of God in this chapter anticipates the ultimate victory of Christ on the cross. Given the apparent advances of evil in our own society – and even in our own lives – how can we live in the reality of Christ's victory?

- Pick up the three main themes we have looked at in the poetry of chapter 3 (the coming, the power and the victory of the Lord) and try either to craft your own poetic summary, or your own prayer of thanksgiving.

# Worship!

## Habakkuk 3:16-19

# Worship!

## INTRODUCTION

In some parts of the world it is now possible to watch interactive movies. Instead of sitting back on the couch and passively watching your favourite film, you are given a remote control and, as the film proceeds, at various points the audience is invited to vote as to which way the plotline will develop. You can decide, for example, whether or not the bad guy gets caught, whether or not the couple will declare their love for each other, or whether it's the maid or the elderly uncle who commits the murder. What the movie makers have discovered is this: people like happy endings. No surprises there. We all love movies that have the happily-ever-after feel to them.

Here we are at the end of the story of Habakkuk. Would you say it's a happy ending? In some senses, yes. There is a note of rejoicing here in these final verses which is hard to miss. But in reality the situation is as bad as ever. It would be a wrong use of language to call this a happy ending, because the situation in which Habakkuk finds himself is as terrifying as it always was. But something has happened to this man along the journey. The song in the closing verses of chapter 3 represents his final response to the overwhelming revelation of God's greatness.

We began in chapter 1 with Habakkuk's bewildered cry – 'Why?' Then in chapter 2, he clambered up the steps of

the city wall and listened for God's word of revelation –
'Wait.' He then heard the revelation in terms of God's
judgement on the Babylonians and on all evil, which we
characterised by the word 'Woe.' And finally he entered
God's presence in prayer and song. The lesson here was to
'Watch' – to see God in his glory and power, to see his
ultimate victory over evil.

It has been a remarkable journey, I hope you'll agree.
And now we come to the closing 4 verses. It is still part of
the song of chapter 3, of course, but it represents his final
response after the overwhelming revelation of God's
greatness. Why, Wait, Woe, Watch and now 'Worship.'

Habakkuk bows the knee to the Sovereign Lord and, in
some of the most moving words in the whole Bible, he
shows us the elements of true worship, the key features of
living a life of faith in this uncertain world. So we have
chosen four headings to summarise the song, which we
will take in the final two chapters of the Study Guide.

# CHAPTER 9

# Respect for the Lord

*Aim: to learn to fear the Lord as we should.*

**FOCUS ON THE THEME**
After all that Habakkuk has witnessed – the sober revelation of judgement and the remarkable vision of the coming of the Lord – he comes to his closing doxology. It is fitting that his first response should be one of godly fear. We will see how a sense of awe is a vital component of true worship for all of God's people.

*Read: Habakkuk 3:16-19*
*Key verse: Habakkuk 3:16*

**Outline**

*Worship!*
Respect for the Lord
Rest in the Lord
Rejoice in the Lord
Rely on the Lord

'I heard and my heart pounded, my lips quivered at the sound; decay crept into my bones and my legs trembled' (v16). If the book of Habakkuk is taught at all in our churches, then usually it is the closing doxology that is selected. And for good reason, for it is one of the most memorable and moving songs in all literature. But sadly, much of the rest of the book is neglected. This is a mistake, since the closing doxology is seen as all the more remarkable, more profoundly moving, in the light of everything that has preceded it. Even those who do preach these closing verses often begin with verse 17, but verse 16 is an integral part of Habakkuk's response. As we have seen, the vision of God's glory in chapter 3 is set within a framework. The two brackets are verses 2 and 16, both saying similar things. 'LORD, I have heard of your fame; I stand in awe of your deeds, O LORD' (v2). He was overwhelmed as he heard the report of God's word. Then he speaks again in verse 16, 'I heard and my heart pounded, my lips quivered at the sound; decay crept into my bones and my legs trembled.'

Having encountered God's majesty and power, having seen God's judgement, he was shaken to the core of his being. Verse 16 describes how he was near to collapse. He trembled like a leaf; he shook from head to toe; he was speechless. Habakkuk records that he felt the impact of this encounter, not simply hearing God's word but now experiencing God himself. In the past he had questioned God about his character, his work and his righteousness. He had appealed for evidence of God's power and of God's control in this uncertain world of his. And now that he had heard, now that he had seen the vision, the revelation from the Lord, he could barely stand up. He was profoundly shaken with a sense of awe, a deep respect for the Lord.

He had got the message. Habakkuk and the people were not going to escape the reality of God's discipline, expressed in the impending judgement brought upon them through the Babylonians. We will see exactly what that discipline meant when we come to verse 17. But for Habakkuk it wasn't simply a reaction of fear, as he thought about the judgement which was to come, though doubtless that contributed to it. His reaction must also have been a response to the extraordinary revelation of God's character that he had just experienced in the vision of chapter 3.

There are many examples in the Bible of a similar reaction on the part of those who came into God's presence. Job's response to the encounter with the living God was, 'I am unworthy.' Like Habakkuk, he was speechless in the face of what God had said and done. Or Isaiah, seeing the throne in Isaiah 6. What was his response? Was he proud that he had been enabled to witness the greatness and the holiness of God? It was quite the reverse. 'Woe to me, I cried, I am ruined. I am a man of unclean lips.'

Every so often in the Gospels there are glimpses of Jesus' own glory and power. Following that incredible fishing expedition, Peter finally said, 'Lord, go away from me. I am a sinful man.' Or another believer who had a profound vision, this time seeing the ascended Christ amongst the lampstands: what was John's response? 'When I saw him, I fell at his feet as though dead.'

In an interesting book called *The Trivialisation of God*, Donald McCullough suggests this:

> Unaccustomed as we are to mystery, we expect nothing even similar to Abraham's falling on his face, Moses' hiding in terror, Isaiah's crying out 'Woe is me', or Saul being knocked flat . . . Reverence and awe have often been replaced by a yawn of familiarity. The consuming fire has been domesticated into a candle flame, adding a bit of religious atmosphere, perhaps but no heat, no blinding light, no power for purification . . . We prefer the illusion of a safer deity and so we have pared God down to manageable proportions.[31]

We can be enormously grateful that in today's evangelicalism we are urged to rejoice in God's grace, to enjoy God's intimacy and to reflect that in joyful informality. But when you read the book of Habakkuk, or some of the other passages to which we have just referred, you realise there is another side to worship, another response that is called for. In our culture, especially in Britain, there are fewer formal expressions of reverence. But the unfortunate result is that such informality also impacts our attitude to God. And as I have looked into my own life, with its inconsistencies and its hypocrisy, and looked again at the fearful majesty of the God to whom this book points, I realise that there are times when I too should tremble, when before God's majestic holiness I should take more than one or two steps back. The God whom we worship is the Lord Almighty, and our worship of him must never lose the element of appropriate awe. He is, as someone has said, the Almighty, not the All-matey.

Peter Lewis, in his excellent book, *The Message of the Living God*, reminds us: 'He is our Father but he is also our holy and heavenly Father, a Father like no other, the Lord, the King. We may not stroll up to him with our hands in our pockets, whistling.'[32]

● *How can we ensure that, in a Christian culture which emphasises informality and intimacy, we can also retain the right sense of awe and godly fear in our lives and our worship?*

## REST IN THE LORD (3:16)

'Yet I will wait patiently for the day of calamity to come on the nation invading us' (v16).

Here is a paradox. In verse 16 he describes how he has collapsed, trembling. But then he continues, 'Yet I will wait patiently . . .' We have noticed this change of mood throughout the book. Do you remember the restless anxiety, the questions, the perplexity of chapter 1? And now here in chapter 3: 'Yet I will wait patiently.' We must remember that the situation hasn't changed. One commentator puts it, 'Nations still rage

. . . the arrogant still rule, the poor still suffer, the enslaved still labour for emptiness and false gods are still worshipped. . .'[33] But Habakkuk knows the One who is working out his purposes, unseen behind the turmoil. Habakkuk knows the end. He knows that God's word is sure, that God's word can be trusted. So now he declares, 'Yet I will wait patiently.' I will rest, because I know that God is true to his promises.

Spurgeon preached a wonderful sermon on these verses. Here is an extract

> We have been assured by people who think they know a great deal about the future that awful times are coming. Be it so; it need not alarm us, for the Lord reigneth. Stay yourself on the Lord . . . and you can rejoice in His name. If the worst comes to the worst, our refuge is in God; if the heavens shall fall the God of heaven will stand; when God cannot take care of His people under heaven, He will take them above the heavens and there they shall dwell with Him. Therefore, as far as you are concerned, rest; for you shall stand . . . at the end of the days.[34]

That captures the spirit of Habakkuk's statement. He knows that God's purposes will be fulfilled. As we saw from the vision given to Habakkuk as he stood on the watchtower, 'The revelation awaits an appointed time; it speaks of an end and will not prove false. Though it linger, wait for it; it will certainly come and will not delay' (Hab. 2:3). We have seen that this represents a primary theme in Habakkuk's prophecy – how to live in the meantime, how to live in the waiting room. Not with anxiety, not with uncertainty, but resting in the sure knowledge that the God who has spoken will bring about his purposes, that the earth will be filled with the knowledge of the glory of God. 'The righteous will live by his faith.'

I hope you see that Habakkuk's story has nothing to do with cheap triumphalism. It certainly hasn't been an easy journey for him. He has been through all kinds of inner turmoil to reach this point of rest in God. Richard Bewes tells the story of Desmond Tutu's response during his struggles in South Africa: 'Sometimes you wish, of course, to say to God, "God, we know that you are in charge, but why don't you make it slightly more obvious?"'

Many of us are asking that question. How was Habakkuk able to rest, to wait patiently? It was his faith in the word of God, that word of revelation. There would be discipline for God's people – he knew that was coming. Both he and Jeremiah had prophesied it and, sure enough, the people were carted off into exile by the Babylonians. We read about it in chapter 1: 'I am raising up the Babylonians, that ruthless and impetuous people, who sweep across the whole earth to seize dwelling-places not their own' (1:6). And now, at the close of his prophecy, Habakkuk points to the inevitable judgement on their enemies too: 'Yet I will wait patiently for the day of calamity to come on the nation invading us' (3:16). Sure enough, Nebuchadnezzar, Belshazzar and all subsequent empires have been judged by God.

Habakkuk had to look through the fog as he wondered about God's purposes and whether God really was in control. But as believers in Jesus Christ we now know what are God's ultimate purposes. We hinted at them as we looked at the theme of the coming of the Lord earlier in Habakkuk 3, and it is expressed in the incredible mission statement that Paul gives in Ephesians. He tells us that God will 'bring all things in heaven and on earth together under one head, even Christ' (Eph. 1:10). So the Christian church must also walk by faith. We too must rest in God's promise and trust in his word as we wait for that final deliverance.

I think we need to pause to ask if that is a reality for us. It might be easier for us to hold on in faith to the ultimate realities we have been describing: trusting God's word that

Jesus will one day return, that his purposes will be fulfilled, that the earth will be filled with the knowledge of the glory of God. But we also need a practical day-by-day faith that keeps on trusting him and holding on to his promises.

Joni Eareckson Tada is well known as a woman who has trusted God through personal tragedy. She once wrote

> Through Kelly's death and my own paralysis I was learning that there was nothing but unhappy frustration in trying to second guess God's purposes. Why God? Why did Kelly die? Why was someone else alive and healthy? There was no reason apart from the overall purposes of God. We aren't always responsible for the circumstances in which we find ourselves; however, we are responsible for the way we respond to them. We can give up, in depression and suicidal despair. Or we can look to a Sovereign God who has everything under control, who can use the experience for our ultimate good by transforming us to the image of Christ.

I found it very helpful to read some words written by Alec Motyer on how we should pray. At first sight you might think that the phrase 'your will be done' imposes a restriction on our praying. But in fact, to pray in this way lifts the restriction. Let's imagine for a moment that God was duty bound to give me everything I ask for. I think that by tomorrow morning I would have stopped praying, because I have no idea what is best for me, my family, my church or my nation. It would be an intolerable burden for a limited, finite mind.[35]

Truly to pray 'your will be done' lifts the restriction of my knowledge. It is to submit to the Lord God Omnipotent, who knows the end from the beginning and who will bring about his good purposes. Habakkuk had learned that this is how he should live: 'your will be done'. Despite all of the turmoil and confusion of Jerusalem, he had learned that God could be trusted. Whatever the future, he could wait on God's purposes. We have seen the Lord's word to Habakkuk in chapter 2: take the long run perspective. And the patient waiting here in 3:16 is part of that same response. Habakkuk could rest in God.

---

## REFLECTION AND RESPONSE

- Habakkuk came to trust God's word. What promises of God are specially helpful to you in learning to rest in him during turbulent times?

- 'Rest in the Lord' might be understood by some people as irresponsible passivity, a kind of 'let go and let God' mentality which dodges human responsibility. How would you reply to that suggestion?

- Can you think of other people in the Bible who learned the same secret as Habakkuk and displayed a similar spirit in the midst of the restless turbulence around them?

- In what ways can we so order our lives that we are regularly reminded of the need to rest in God? Can any member of the group give an example of simple things which have enabled them to focus on these realities?

CHAPTER 10

# Rejoice in the Lord

*Aim: to entrust our life and our world to the Sovereign Lord.*

**FOCUS ON THE THEME**
At the close of Habakkuk's journey, this man of faith finally responds with a joyful acknowledgement that, even if all else is stripped away, he has the Lord himself, on whom he could completely rely.

*Read: Habakkuk 3:16-19*
*Key verse: Habakkuk 3:17,18*

**Outline**

*Worship!*
Respect for the Lord
Rest in the Lord
Rejoice in the Lord
Rely on the Lord

'Yet I will rejoice in the LORD, I will be joyful in God my Saviour' (v18). What is so moving about this song of worship is the context in which it is sung. There is a danger that, given the familiarity and the beauty of the poetry, we miss the force of the implications of verse 17: 'Though the fig tree does not bud and there are no grapes on the vines, though the olive crop fails and the fields produce no food, though there are no sheep in the pen and no cattle in the stalls, yet I will rejoice ...'

What is Habakkuk describing in that verse? It is possible that he is anticipating the ultimate Day of the Lord. But it is also highly likely that he is describing the devastating impact of the predicted coming invasion of the Babylonian war machine that was described in chapter 1.

The verse is clear: everything has been taken away. David Prior expresses it like this: 'the ravages of war, the horrors of invasion, the devastation of nature's resources, the removal of all basic necessities.'[36] That's what is described in verse 17. It begins with the apparent luxuries of figs, grapes, olives but then the verse moves very quickly to show that there is no food at all. It wasn't simply a devastated economic and social infrastructure. *Everything* had gone.

Perhaps you have seen on TV the thousands of shacks of desperate people living in the slums of Africa or Asia. If you have visited them, you will know how devastating is the impact. You can't stand and take photos; you are overwhelmed by the smell, the ill-dressed children, the filth of what passes for homes, the meals on which they barely survive. But what Habakkuk is describing is more extreme still. As David Prior expresses it, 'it is Bosnia, Vietnam and Rwanda rolled into one.'[37]

That's what makes this small word 'Yet' all the more remarkable. He is stripped of everything and still this man of faith sings 'Yet I will rejoice in the LORD.' 'Yet I will wait patiently' (v16); 'Yet I will rejoice' (v18). It is Job saying, 'Though he slay me, yet I will hope in him.' It is Paul saying 'We are hard pressed on every side, but not crushed.'

There is another famous doxology, found in Job chapter 1. Job had received the devastating news of a catalogue of disasters: his oxen, donkeys, sheep and camels had all been taken away. All of his servants had been killed and all of his children had died when the house collapsed on them. Satan's wager with God was, 'Stretch out your hand and strike everything he has and he will surely curse you to your face' (Job 1:11). And what was Job's response? '"Naked I came from my mother's womb, and naked I will depart. The LORD gave and the LORD has taken away; may the name of the LORD be praised." In all of this, Job did not sin by charging God with wrongdoing' (Job 1:21,22). So instead of cursing God, Job the man of faith blessed the Lord.

Again, it's very important to see those words in their context. This is no cheap Hallelujah. Warren Wiersbe, commenting on the Job phrase says, 'Anybody can say, "The Lord gave" or "The Lord has taken away" but it takes real faith to say in the midst of sorrow and suffering, "Blessed be the name of the Lord."'[38]

## REJOICE IN THE LORD! (3:17,18)

How can Habakkuk respond as he does? The key is in verse 18. What was there left for Habakkuk to rejoice in? It was not his possessions; it was certainly not his circumstances. It was not what we might call the blessings of God. They are not there in verse 17. It was 'Rejoice in the Lord.' Like Job, he was stripped of everything else but God. And that is the key to his joy; it is finding that God the Creator, the Redeemer, the covenant-keeping God is enough. That is how Habakkuk concludes his prophecy. All of those things on which we rely may be stripped away, but God is enough. And yet I wonder: can this reality, the reality of God himself, be enough for us?

All we have seen in the book of Habakkuk points us to this fact: for men and women of faith, evil has lost the initiative. When we become Christians we do not automatically beam up into the mothership. We are not protected from the hardships of this world. There is no guarantee that we will be immune from suffering or from God's discipline, from the oppression of enemies, or from the pains and dangers of living in this broken world. But we know that the Lord will not let go of his people, that he has not abandoned his world. He is still in control and his purposes will be fulfilled. People of faith, like Habakkuk, come to realise that, since we have God, we have enough. 'Yet I will rejoice in the Lord, I will joy in the God of my salvation.'

It is important that I am not misunderstood here. There was a time when books were published about the secrets of 'praise power.' John White calls them the 'cruel merchants of praise power' and Richard Foster wrote, 'In its worst form this teaching denies the vileness of evil and baptises the most horrible tragedies as the will of God. Scripture commands us to live in a spirit of thanksgiving in the midst of all situations; it does not command us to celebrate the presence of evil.'[39] Whatever the source of the difficulty, whether Satanic in origin as Job found, or simply the result of living in a fractured and fallen world, ultimately all of these things are within the sovereign purposes of God. And that's what Habakkuk came to see.

I was recently with a group of leaders in Albania and I met a remarkable Christian from Kosovo who is now helping the small churches there. He used to run a number of businesses in Kosovo before the war, and he was very successful. He had several shops and a couple of houses and he became quite famous – he was a bodybuilder who eventually became the Yugoslav weightlifting champion. When Kosovo was invaded, he was forced to evacuate the shops. He left his home, he was beaten up, and his family was taken away as refugees. He went in search of them and eventually he found them in Albania. Whilst he was there he came across a small Christian mission which provided food. Eventually the family returned to Kosovo. He looked for his shops, only to discover they had been completely destroyed. He returned to his two homes but they had both been burned down. And then as he was walking through the city, he saw a white van with a fish sign on the back and he recognised the same Christians he had met in Albania. Eventually, through their help, he came to faith in Christ. And he said to me through the translator, 'I had nothing, but I have now found everything. *The Lord is my life.*'

I think there would be many reading these words, or many in our local church, who could echo that sentiment. Some have lost partners or children, some have journeyed through dark valleys, but they have discovered that Habakkuk's song rings true. When everything is taken away, the Lord is my life. 'I will rejoice in God.' That is the song of the true believer, confirmed through the work of our Lord Jesus, who 'for the joy set before him, endured the cross, despising its shame and is now seated at the right hand of the Father.'

● *Habakkuk was able to rejoice when everything was stripped away, because his joy was in God alone. What does 'rejoicing' look like when it is in the midst of trouble? Can you think of Christians who have demonstrated this?*

## RELY ON THE LORD (3:19)

Here is the fourth key to Habakkuk's worship and his life of faith. Look at verse 19, 'The Sovereign LORD is my strength; he makes my feet like the feet of a deer, he enables me to go on to the heights.' Earlier we suggested that one of the important disciplines when life looks as though it is out of control is to remember the certainties. 'My God, my holy one, we will not die' (Hab. 1:12). And just as in his first chapter, now in the closing verses Habakkuk does the same, doubtless with added vigour: 'I will be joyful in God *my Saviour'* (v18); 'the Sovereign LORD is *my* strength' (v19). He knows that he will never be separated from the covenant God, whatever is going on in the world around him. God is my strength. God is my rock.

It is precisely in these moments of pressure that we come to know the Lord in ways we would never otherwise have done. We are forced to trust him more than we would have done if life had been relatively straightforward.

Jim Packer, in his wonderful book *Knowing God,* has a chapter called 'These inward trials'.

> How does God prosecute this purpose? Not by shielding us from assault by the world, the flesh and the devil, not by protecting us from burdensome and frustrating circumstances, nor yet by shielding us from troubles created by our own temperament and psychology; but rather by exposing us to all these things, so as to overwhelm us with a sense of our own inadequacy and to drive us to cling to Him more closely. This is the ultimate reason, from our standpoint, why God fills our lives with troubles and perplexities of one sort and another – it is to ensure that we shall learn to hold Him fast.[40]

The Lord is my strength – the Hebrew word could also mean 'army.' The Lord is my army, the One who sustains my life, the life of the 'righteous who live by faith.' He provides for the person who might have lost everything else, the person who has been pushed right to the limits. God the Lord is my strength. He is all I need.

It is similar to Paul's well-known testimony in 2 Corinthians 12. Frequently Paul had prayed for the removal of his thorn in the flesh. And how did the Lord reply? 'My grace is sufficient for you, for my power is made perfect in weakness.' It was an unexpected answer to his prayer which became 'the most powerful inspiration of his life.' Now God's all-sufficient grace was poured into his life, not in spite of the thorn but because of that very weakness. 'The Sovereign Lord is my strength.' The breakthrough for Paul was to see that weakness has the special advantage of making room for God's grace. It is when God can work most effectively, when his power can be most clearly seen.

It was just the same in Jeremiah's experience. He confronted a range of challenges, just like Habakkuk. He was God's opposition spokesman, confronting the priests, the military and the politicians. But in the midst of his call to service we discover some significant strong assurances. God promises that he will be a fortified city, an iron pillar, a bronze wall (Jer. 1:18). They are very graphic descriptions, perhaps also expressing his loneliness. But God was giving him a strength that would enable him to accept his weakness and fears and still stand up to the world.

Habakkuk's testimony included that kind of commitment. He is now sure-footed. There is both stability and energy: 'He enables me to go on the heights' (v19). So as I put my faith in him, I can live with 'unstumbling security', rising above all of the oppression of the world. God enables his people to keep walking, to keep climbing.

David Prior makes the legitimate point that many of us experience what he describes as 'spiritual vertigo.' We grow queasy at the thought of some of the spiritual challenges, the mountains which lie ahead of us. Our legs begin to buckle when we think about threatening circumstances. So the result is that we live our lives within cautiously safe limits. But God 'enables me to go on the heights' (v19). Habakkuk had confronted many high places and there were still more mountains ahead too. But through his encounter with the living God, he now knew he could rise above those challenges because God had equipped him: 'He enables me' (v19).

When I travel to the English Lake District, I often think of Psalm 121. 'I lift up my eyes to the hills – where does my help come from? My help comes from the LORD, the Maker of heaven and earth.' My colleague, Chris Wright, heard an African preacher expound that Psalm like this. 'I look to the hills and I think: However am I going to do it? It's impossible. Look at that mountain!' That's the opposite of how I had understood it. I see the mountain and I think, 'How beautiful, how inspiring!' But the African preacher thought of it quite differently. 'This mountain is impossible, so as I look to the hills I think, where is my help going to come from?' And so verse 2 follows, 'My help comes from the LORD, the Maker of heaven and earth.' He is the one who enables me to climb this mountain. And that was Habakkuk's testimony. Whatever mountains he faced, he could rely on the Lord.

Some writers also remind us of another possible implication of the expression 'the heights' in verse 19. This refers to the high places which were under the control of hostile forces. I was recently travelling in northern India and journeyed over several mountain passes. At the top, travellers find religious shrines, for very often the 'high places' are the centres of pagan worship. It's often symbolic, as it was in the Old Testament. The gods, they thought, controlled the high ground and were therefore in charge of the whole area.

So is it possible that Habakkuk means that God enables us to go even into those heights, those spiritual territories, those high places of the enemy? By God's power, by God's word and by God's Spirit, he enables us to see the gospel advance whatever the situation, whatever hostile forces may be ranged against Christ and against his people. He enables me to go on to those very heights.

## REVIEW OF SECTION 5

We have focused on the four keys to Habakkuk's worship and his life of faith. They are

- respect for the Lord
- rest in the Lord
- rejoice in the Lord
- rely on the Lord

This has been Habakkuk's journey: from the confusion of chapter 1 to the confidence of chapter 3, from Why to Worship. He had not only understood a theological proposition that God was in charge of world affairs, but he had come to realise it in the depth of his being. In our uncertain world, this must become our confidence too: the assurance that God can be trusted to do what is right, that nothing will hinder his good purposes and that we can entrust our life, our world and our future to him. Habakkuk would affirm Paul's majestic conclusion

> We know that in all things God works for the good of those who love him, who have been called according to his purpose . . . Who shall separate us from the love of Christ? Shall trouble or hardship or persecution or famine or nakedness or danger or sword? As it is written; 'For your sake we face death all day long; we are considered as sheep to be slaughtered.' No, in all these things we are more than conquerors through him who loved us. For I am convinced that neither death nor life, neither angels nor demons, neither the present nor the future, nor any powers, neither height nor depth, nor anything else in all creation, will be able to separate us from the love of God that is in Christ Jesus our Lord (Rom. 8:28,35-39).

## REFLECTION AND RESPONSE

- Do you suffer from spiritual vertigo? Are you in danger of living life within cautiously safe limits, and are there some 'mountains' ahead that you know you should tackle in God's strength?

- The psalmist expresses the same confidence and trust as Habakkuk, when he records his testimony in Psalm 73:25,26. Use this as a prayer, asking the Lord to make this true in your own life.

## FURTHER STUDY

Compare Habakkuk 3:17,18 with Psalm 144:13-15. Is the Old Testament somehow inconsistent?

# ENDNOTES

1   James Martin, *The Meaning of the 21st Century* (Eden Project books, 2006), p3
2   D. Martyn Lloyd-Jones, *From Fear to Faith* (IVP, 1953), pp16-18, (re-issued 2003)
3   David Atkinson, *The Message of Job* (IVP, 1991), p22
4   Quoted in Ivan Klima, *Between Security and Insecurity* (Thames & Hudson, 1999), p38
5   J.I. Packer, *Knowing God* (Hodder & Stoughton, 1973), p228
6   John Goldingay, *God's Prophet, God's Servant* (Carlisle: Paternoster Press, 1984)
7   John Goldingay, *Songs from a Strange Land* (IVP, 1978), p34
8   D. Martyn Lloyd-Jones, *Spiritual Depression* (Eerdmans, 1965)
9   C.S. Lewis, *Mere Christianity* (Fontana, 1954), p121
10  Thomas Friedman, *Longitudes and Attitudes* (Anchor/Random House, 2003), pp17,18
11  Don Carson, *A Call to Spiritual Reformation* (Leicester: IVP, 1992), pp36,37
12  David Prior, *The Message of Joel, Micah and Habakkuk* (IVP, 1988), p233
13  Quoted in Elizabeth Achtemeier, *Interpretation (Nahum to Malachi)* (John Knox Press 1986)
14  John White, *The Fight* (IVP, 1977), pp54,55
15  Eugene Peterson, *Run With the Horses* (Downers Grove: IVP, 1983), p54
16  Harry Blamires, *The Christian Mind* (SPCK, 1963)
17  J.I. Packer, op.cit, p125
18  David Atkinson, op.cit, p244
19  Theo Latsch, quoted in Richard D. Patterson, *The Wycliffe Exegetical Commentary, Nahum, Habakkuk, Zephaniah* (Chicago: Moody Press, 1991), p194
20  Bryan Appleyard, article in *The Times*, 'Are you sinning comfortably?', April 11 2004
21  op. cit
22  *Jesus shall reign* by Isaac Watts, 1674-1748
23  David Bryant, *In the Gap* (Downers Grove: IVP, 1981)

24 *All my hope on God is founded* by Robert Seymour Bridges, 1844-1930, based on Joachim Neander, 1650-80

25 Quoted in Mark Buchanan, *The Holy Wild* (Multnomah, 2003), p28

26 D.A. Carson, *A Call to Spiritual Reformation* (IVP, 1992), p15

27 Mark Meynell, *Cross-examined* (IVP, 2001), p72

28 John R.W. Stott, *The Cross of Christ* (IVP, 2006)

29 J.I. Packer, op.cit. pp77,78

30 David Atkinson, op.cit, p156

31 Donald McCullough, quoted in Peter Lewis, *The Message of the Living God* (IVP, 2000), pp320,321

32 Peter Lewis, op.cit

33 Elizabeth Achtemeier, op.cit, p58

34 Quoted in Elizabeth Achtemeier, op.cit, p60

35 J.A. Motyer, *The Tests of Faith* (Leicester: IVP, 1970), pp117,118

36 David Prior, op.cit, p275

37 David Prior, op.cit, p275

38 Warren W. Wiersbe, *Be Patient* (Scripture Press, 1992), p18

39 Richard Foster, *Celebration of Discipline* (Hodder & Stoughton, 1978), p166

40 J.I. Packer, op.cit, p227